When Prince Charming Falls off His Horse

. . . and you've become his nag!

by
Becky Yates Spencer

with comments by Tracy Spencer

with comments by Tracy Spencer

Photograph of Becky and Tracy provided by Monica Warren.

Back cover photograph provided by David Boman.

Front cover art & cover design by Daniel Nowlan.

First printing November 2003

Library of Congress Control Number: 2003098695

ISBN: 0-9747561-0-5

Printed in the U.S.A. by
Morris Publishing
3212 East Highway 30
Kearney, NE 68847
1-800-650-7888

This book is lovingly dedicated to my mother,
Pattie Yates Belden,
who taught me by example
what commitment really meant.

Mama, Tracy and I are forever grateful!

Empty, lonely,

Longing to be loved;

Broken, dying,

Hearing You're the One.

Reaching, pleading,

Asking You to fill my dreams,

Believing, receiving,

Finding You're the God Who meets my needs.

By Becky Spencer

Acknowledgements

As with most major undertakings, the writing of this book has only come to fruition thanks to the efforts of many people who were willing to pitch in and share their time and talents.

First, I want to thank my editors. Pastor Jim Francis, thank you for faithfully dividing the Word of truth and sharing that discernment with my readers! Even Annie added her scribbles, evidence of a dad who knows how to balance more than the Scriptures! Multi-tasking, right? Liz and Geoff D'Urso, you thoroughly savored each word and concept to grasp the meaning I was after, and your comments back to me were just as precise. You even gave up your Sunday afternoon nap for this chore! We are talking MAJOR sacrifice of love here, and I owe you! Coleen Yocum, you are the BEST cheerleader a gal could ever hope for! Your encouragement always makes me believe I can accomplish any task, while your love makes me want to give my very best! Mama (Pattie Yates Belden to the rest of you!), after living through most of this story with me, I know the reading of it was not always easy. Your advice then helped me get through it; now your literary expertise is helping me tell it. Invaluable! Carol Wagner, once an English teacher, always an English teacher! You caught things that slipped right by everyone else—and didn't even use a red pen once!

Next, several people helped get the cover done. Danny Nowlan, when you were my student, I knew you were talented; now as my son-in-law, you've also proven you're *patient* by tackling this design project! I'm thankful Sara realized you are a keeper! Pam Vieyra, you saved me with your quick computer skills! Mama was right—you really CAN do anything! Doug Hanna, you gave up your Sunday afternoon and shooed your company away early to let me into the computer lab, too, even running errands for me while I typed. You have such a servant's heart that the Lord will use around the world! Seth, I think Doug is a genius, and he thinks YOU are, so that speaks for itself! Thanks for letting me use your "stuff"!

D.L, you have waited patiently for this book to finally be in print, and your generosity made it possible! I'm convinced that in eternity you will have a long line of women who are waiting to thank you for the sacrifices you made to get this teaching into their hands. Hulse and Carol, you contributed at a desperate time when I absolutely HAD to get out of the house to write where it was quiet! Thank you for that crucial gift that came on the perfect weekend!

Tracy and all my children, once again you have patiently worked around me and eaten macaroni and cheese or bean burritos or take-out too many nights to count so I could finish this project. You weathered the inevitable stresses that come with living with a writer, and you still loved me when I was done! You also sacrificed your privacy so this story could be told. I am more proud of you than words can say.

To my MANY prayer warriors who saw this book to completion, you deserve HUGE applause! The last month of editing brought more opposition than we would have dreamed possible, but you fought the good fight of faith and covered me with your prayers so I could focus and finish. We started with a core group of fifty people, but the prayer requests circled the globe. I didn't even know all of you, but Jesus knows your names and your heart! He promises that if you give a prophet a cup of water in His Name, you will receive the reward of a prophet, and I know that any victories won in the lives of people who take the truths of this book to heart will be credited to your heavenly accounts!

Jesus, YOU ARE MY PRINCE and I eagerly await your return! Thank you for providing all I need to be a bride adorned without spot or wrinkle! See you at the wedding feast!

Contents

Introduction: It All Started Long, Long Ago 11

1. Someday My Prince Will Come 13
2. The Wonderful Kingdom of Shackri-la 29
3. Queen Jezebel 33
4. Camelot 37
5. Throwing a Royal Fit 62
6. King of the Castle? 72
7. There Are Dragons Out There! 84
8. Granting a Royal Pardon 102
9. A Kingdom Divided 110
10. There's a Draft in the Castle (an overdraft, that is!) 134
11. The Middle Ages (or "The Old Gray Mare, She Ain't What She Used to Be!") 145
12. Damsel in Distress 157
13. A Mighty Fortress . . . Is Our God 172
14. Happily Ever After 181

Photo 189

Appendix: The King's Proclamation 191

Suggested Reading 195
Ordering/Booking Information 197

It All Started Long, Long Ago

(Okay, this is really the Introduction, but if I'd said that, you might have skipped it! You need to read this part, so please, just take a few seconds to run through this, okay? Thanks!)

Every girl dreams of someday finding her one and only—the love of her life, her knight in shining armor, her Prince Charming who will sweep her off her feet, deposit her in front of him on his valiant steed, and ride off into the sunset to live happily ever after.

The only problem with that scenario is that it doesn't exist! Women continue to dream and hope generation after generation, only to discover that reality is a completely different picture.

Why does a woman have that kind of hope and dream in her heart if it can never come true for her? Why would it be part of her innate makeup if it were unattainable from the minute she begins to have stars in her eyes? Is it a cruel joke or a trap to give her disappointment and grief all the days of her life? Is it intended to bring her up, only to slam her down into despair time after time?

I can say, without a doubt, that our heavenly Father did NOT have that in mind when He created man and woman! Certainly, we see or know or ARE one of many women who move from one relationship to another, looking for the kind of love that will bring fulfillment and happiness at last. In today's culture, we even see women who have become disillusioned with men to the point of turning to other women for love and acceptance. Unfortunately, it is a vain attempt to fill a void—one that our Creator never intended to be filled by another human being.

I believe that every person has a deeply ingrained desire to be courted, wooed, won, and loved eternally. That's because God created us to be intimate with Him! He "wired" us to need someone else so we would seek love. The relationship between a woman and a man is meant to mirror the type of love God planned for us, but it was *never* intended to be the main emphasis. A mirror merely reflects the true image! God longs to give us the love, acceptance, and contentment we long for—and He's the *only* One capable of doing so completely!

We make ourselves miserable and set ourselves up for disappointment when we try to fill that deep spiritual need in a relationship with another person. It simply can't be done! We place unrealistic expectations on another human being to make us happy, keep us content, and meet our needs. Unfair! Impossible! Disappointing!

So why even marry at all then, you might ask! If the marriage relationship is not intended to meet our deepest needs, what is the purpose? Should we all lower our expectations and settle for a slob drinking beer in front of the television? Should we find escape in romance novels or soap operas or Hollywood's version of happiness?

I have found that there is more—MUCH more! In the writing of this book, I simply want to share my story. It is one of ignorance, selfishness, temptation, hatred, grief and despair. Yet it is also one of commitment that eventually led to hope and joy and unconditional love. It is one of a journey that is far from over, one that is full of new discoveries. It is not a recipe for happiness, a marriage manual, a promise of easy answers, or a way to make your spouse change. It is simply my story! My prayer is that through reading it, you will be encouraged to look to Jesus in a fresh way and that you will have your hope renewed.

Even with all the Lord has taught me through the years, I certainly don't have all the answers, and I'll undoubtedly say the wrong thing somewhere along the way. But my goal is to point you to Jesus as you read this text, because He not only has all the answers—*He is love*!

So keep reading—you'll find that there IS a Prince concerned with every longing heart!

1. Someday My Prince Will Come

The typical story goes something like this: boy meets girl, they fall in love, they marry, and they live happily ever after. Stuff fairy tales are made of, to be sure, but NOT the experience of the majority of relationships! Mine was unique in that I didn't even fall in love before marrying my husband, Tracy! Let me back up and tell how our marriage came to be, which actually can be best understood by going back to my childhood.

My earliest memories of my dad are of a handsome, suave young man with a macho attitude! His dark hair was combed neatly into a ducktail, and he walked with confidence—not the businessman kind of clip, but a swagger that showed he knew who he was and everyone else would do well to realize it, too. He was cool—the James Dean "Rebel Without a Cause" kind of cool that got results!

My mother was vivacious and beautiful—definitely up to the task of keeping up with Daddy! I loved to hear stories of what it was like when they met. She was the third in a line-up of ten children, and her father had passed away when she was only eight years old. Because of problems at home in her early teen years, she moved from Okmulgee, Oklahoma, to a farm near Alden, Kansas, to live with her Aunt Esther. When she met my father, she decided right away that she was going to marry him, and she did when she was only fifteen years old and he was sixteen. They lived with his parents at first on the family farm in Sterling, Kansas.

Daddy started drinking at an early age, and he didn't stop after marrying Mama, nor after we kids came along. I was born first of six children, so I remember his various jobs, like his working in the oil fields when I was very small and his farming for a while. For several years he was a long-distance truck driver for Allied Van Lines Moving Company, often gone for weeks at a time. Mama was the stability of our home and the glue that held us together when Daddy was coming loose at the seams.

He was bigger than life, taking up all the space in a room when he entered. He was like a magnet and could tell stories that held us spell-bound. Never mind that the topic was often about the fights he got into at the bars! There were also stories of incidents from his childhood, and I craved learning all I could about my grandparents and their way of life. His mother, my Grandma Yates, could also weave a captivating story, and my favorite times were Sunday afternoons when three or four generations of our family would get together for dinner and an afternoon of sharing. We heard the same stories over and over, but it never got old; it was comforting just to be together with some semblance of normal family life.

Even though there are some bad memories of my childhood, my parents always made a point to tell us that they loved us. There were so many good things along with the bad. For instance, Mom and Dad encouraged me to bond with my grandparents and often took us to the farm to visit with them. And my mother was amazing: when Daddy would go drinking on Friday nights, she would come home from the store with Jiffy popcorn—the kind we used to shake over the burner on the stove! She bought Pepsi, which was a real treat, and sometimes she'd get those little colored tablets that we'd put in the bottom of our water glasses to make a fizzy drink. She made homemade pizza for us on some of those Friday nights, or other times she fried hamburgers, and she made sure that we were building good memories as a family, even when her own life was hard.

She always took us to church on Sunday mornings, too. I can still see our sofa on Saturday, where she was laying out our pressed dresses and Sunday socks and shoes so that we could get ready on time the next morning. She polished our shoes bright white and put those pink spongy curlers in our hair, doing her best to make us presentable, even though she didn't have much money or help from Daddy.

Saturdays were also spent cleaning the house. The worst part of that was when we didn't know where Daddy was. I'd get a ball in the pit of my stomach, fear that was growing into something almost tangible. I would throw myself into dusting and polishing and sweeping, and after I was old enough, helping with the ironing. I loved the Pepsi bottle with a little metal attachment on the top, full of holes so we could sprinkle water on the clothes before pressing them with the hot iron! My worry about Daddy gave me energy to keep working hard, but even then, Mama made the day more tolerable by playing all kinds of music. I would dream and dance around the house, pretending to be a ballerina or a famous singer or movie star. Mama fed the best dreams in us, always making us believe that no matter what our circumstances were, we could accomplish whatever we set our minds to.

There were good memories of Daddy, too, like of his getting down on all fours and chasing us kids, roaring like a lion. We would scream and run under the dining room table to hide, the delicious combination of fear and excitement mingling while we waited for him to catch us! When he did, he'd tickle us till we nearly cried; then the game would start over again. What fond memories!

We went on family picnics at Carey Park, stopping near the park entrance to see the fountain with its rainbow of colors on hot summer nights. Sometimes we were then surprised with a trip to Dairy Queen for a chocolate push-up.

Not all of my memories were good, though, any more than anyone else's are about childhood. The unpleasant times were when Daddy came home drunk. I would wake up and creep out to make sure my mother was okay, because he was often loud. Not only did he tell us about his fights, but sometimes he also reenacted them for us, swaying and swinging at invisible ruffians in the dark. One night while he was "performing," his wedding ring came off his finger and slid across the floor. I left my spot on the sofa to get it for him, but my mother shouted at me to sit back down. She knew that he wouldn't ever hurt me intentionally, but he was lost in an oblivious world of his own making.

I faced disappointment at one of my early birthday parties he missed because he was drinking, and I was distracted from really enjoying the party because I was watching for him to arrive.

There were also memories of his getting sick under the kitchen table, unable even to pick up his head from the mess or crawl to the bathroom. There was the terror of seeing him pick up my mother by her nightgown, ripping it as he threatened her. There was shouting and arguing from behind their closed bedroom door, usually the day after one of his binges.

The worst time, though, was one Saturday when he was going to leave us. I can still see him with his jaw set and his suitcase packed. Mama stood by silently, not making him leave, but also not standing in his way to prevent him. When I realized he was really going to do it, I began to scream for him not to go. I clung to his pant legs, and he dragged me along as he walked out to the car. Between my sobs, I was begging him not to leave—I thought I'd die if he went away. When he couldn't keep me peeled off, because I just kept reattaching myself, he finally came back in the house. I don't know what conversation took place between my parents, but he stayed home after all. Even as horrid as things were at times, I couldn't stand the thought of being without him.

In spite of the heartache associated with Daddy's drinking, my parents taught us to know the difference between right and wrong. I can still recall my fear the time they lined us kids up to try to discover who had taken a $5 bill from Daddy's wallet. I was the one! They forgave me and loved me and taught me, and it sure never happened again!

For as long as I can remember, I just wanted Daddy's attention and approval and love. That didn't change, not for as long as he lived; I don't think it will completely change for as long as *I* live, either. There were some rough years when I tried to find those things from other males since I didn't think I had them from him.

Speaking of males, I always liked boys and got along with them, often better than I got along with girls. I remember having "boyfriends" clear back in elementary school. I can vividly remember sitting on the monkey bars with another girl, sharing with the world in our sing-song voices as we clapped out a rhythm, "My boyfriend's name is Tony; he came from the land of baloney, with pickles on his nose and mustard on his toes; my boyfriend's name is Tony!" And wouldn't you know it, there was actually a boy named Tony in my fifth grade class, so I had a real live target as the object of my affection! There was no end to my dreams of what life would be like with Tony. The white picket fence vision started early for me, including how many children we would have (twins, a boy and a girl), what I would name them (Heath and Heather), and how their chubby faces would break into grins when their daddy came home from whatever it was he did all day to make a living for us! In my dream, his arrival would take place with the twins playing inside the fence while I hung our sparkling laundry out on the clothesline, its fresh scent billowing to greet him as I pushed aside my wavy brown hair and smiled up at him, waiting for my hello kiss. Naturally, the birds sang and butterflies flitted nearby, perfectly content to linger in our loving atmosphere!

By the time I finished junior high, my dad had quit drinking for the most part. He had gone through a surgery on his foot that ended up becoming infected, so he was in isolation in the hospital for an additional seventeen days. My mother's cousin Hal spent time talking to Daddy about the love of Jesus Christ, and Daddy opened his heart to a genuine experience with Jesus that made a difference in his life. Our family would sometimes sing specials at church together during the months after his hospitalization, and my favorite was "Standing on the Promises." That was truly what I did to get through; I relied on the promises of God. Even though I wasn't familiar with much of the Bible, the hymns of the faith beat strongly in my heart, and I would sing them for hours at a time, finding courage and comfort in the truth of the words. The Lord's presence became real to me as I lifted my praise.

Junior high brought even more interest in boys, but my severe acne caused me to withdraw a lot. Still, there were boys who were on my level socially, and they didn't seem to mind that my appearance was far from perfect. I lived in a melodramatic world, and each relationship was lived as though I were watching myself on a movie screen. The boys involved didn't seem to notice that I was the star of the production going on in my head. I remember one day stopping by a young man's house. It was summer, so school was out, and he lived in our neighborhood. I was "going with him," which was the terminology used for what had been called "going steady" in my mother's time, and what is now called "going out" in my kids' day. It really didn't mean much except that we gained some sort of shaky confidence that someone else found us attractive and desirable.

On this particular day, a storm began to blow in and the wind was really picking up. I thought I'd better get home before it got really bad out, especially because I carried some responsibility for my younger siblings. I dramatically kissed this boy goodbye, telling him that I must hurry home before the storm hit! I was on stage, acting out the drama of our goodbye, which could possibly be our last one, since the coming storm could end it all for us! Our parting was full of bittersweet passion as we tore ourselves apart in the street before I ran home. We didn't get blown away, though, and when that relationship was over within the month, I was on to another one!

In high school, though, I dated more seriously, as most of us do. My mother had taken me to a dermatologist, so my face was clearing up some. A friend had convinced me to try out for choir and school plays, and my confidence was growing as I found success singing and acting.

By this time, Daddy was only drinking once or twice a year, usually when my mother was out of town. His personality still exhibited many of the characteristics of an addictive person, though. He was demanding and critical, with a temper that flared at the slightest offense. If my mother was just a few minutes later than he thought she should be, he wanted to know where she'd been, whom she'd seen and talked to, and so on. During one particularly bad time I remember vowing to my mother that I would never let a man treat me that way. Little did I know how binding and strong those words would be and how they would come back to haunt me.

At fifteen years old, I met the cutest boy yet during a camping trip to Kanopolis Lake with my family. His family was also there, and both families seemed to approve of our friendship. Randy was a Boy Scout, clean cut, and amazingly, liked me! We have an 8 mm home film of my gangly attempts to play softball with him and our siblings and a few other kids who were also camping. We laughed and talked and shared, and I was smitten! He lived in Wichita and we were in Hutchinson, so only an hour separated us. Our families began to plan activities together from time to time, and we dated "long distance" for about a year and a half. My family joined his for his Eagle Scout pinning, and his family camped in our back yard for a fun-filled weekend together. We held hands and stole kisses while our love grew, and we began to talk seriously about getting married. The promises we made to each other about our future were fervent, and I was sure we would spend our lives together. The dreams from childhood continued in my mind, only the face coming to greet me in the yard simply changed.

My junior year, however, we had planned to attend Snowball together at my high school. It was the winter dance, and my pop choir was performing. My mother had a beautiful purple velvet skirt made for me, along with a flocked floral top. She made an appointment for my hair to be done at the salon, and it was piled high atop my head. (Naturally, I hated it! Ha!)

The weather began to turn bad, but I never dreamed anything would keep Randy away. After I got home from the salon, though, his father phoned to say that Randy would not be able to come, due to the snowy, icy roads. I couldn't believe my ears! Surely a little snow wouldn't keep my love away! I figured that if the mailman couldn't be deterred by inclement weather, love certainly needed to do better than that! His dad's words were final, though, and there was nothing I could do about it. I ran to my room, flung myself over my bed, and wailed until my mother finally thought I had carried on long enough. She tried to cheer me up and get me to see reason, but I was beyond help. She reminded me that nobody had *died*, but I was in a role! I had to act out every emotion of the drama, and this one called for inconsolable grief!

I ended up calling a friend in pop choir, offering him the two tickets to the dance for free. He said he would take me, but I wouldn't allow myself to be persuaded. I brushed through my hair to try to flatten it a little, tried to do something about my puffy, red face, and then spent the evening after our performance with my two best friends who consoled me with A & W root beer, hamburgers, and their humor. Something changed in my relationship with Randy, though, and I ended up breaking up with him. I wanted to have someone to share all the fun things at school with, and it seemed that the dream was falling apart. Since reality didn't match my fantasy, I moved on. Later I learned that I had hurt him terribly, and the time would come when I would be sorry for that, but for the moment, all I was concerned with was my own happiness.

That should have been a clue, because love is supposed to be something we GIVE to someone else. But so often when we say, "I love you," what we really mean is, "I need you to meet certain longings in me, and I'll give in to you only to the point I have to in order to get what I'm really wanting." Scary and sad, but in my case, I was just looking for something and someone who would make ME feel special. I didn't have a clue about what real love was, so the search continued.

My senior year of high school, I began dating another boy seriously. This young man was all I'd dreamed of as he opened doors for me, took me out to eat, remembered special days with yellow roses, and treated me like a lady in every way. Just like with Randy, we also dated for about a year and a half, and I was building brand new memories and dreams with him. He wasn't even the dreamy, good-looking sort of fellow I'd always fallen for before, but his manners and chivalry more than made up for any lack in that department. We decided we would marry, and I was enjoying receiving the attention I had longed for all my life.

I was willing to give this young man all of myself, and eventually, that is what he asked of me. The summer after graduation, while he was on harvest for his uncle, I went to visit him and spent the night, giving myself to him sexually, trying to convince myself that our love would make it okay. Although I was not equipped with the Truth that would help me avoid sexual entanglement, I still realized that it was wrong to sleep together without being married. I wanted to please him and be together so much, though, that I tried to push aside my guilt. I moved into a studio apartment so that we could have more time together, and we both enrolled in classes at the community college.

Although as a young person I had promised myself I would never drink alcohol since it had caused so much pain in our family, I began to drink with this boyfriend. He would bring a bottle of wine to my apartment, and sometimes he would also invite some friends from the community theatre over. I always planned to have just one drink, but I ended up drunk every time. My life was a roller coaster—one minute bliss, as he seemed to show me such care and concern, the next minute misery as I realized how low I was sinking morally.

Our sin caused me to miss the presence of God in my life, even though I didn't have a deep relationship with Him, so I asked my boyfriend if we could start going to church together. He agreed, but somehow sleeping together on Saturday night, then attending church on Sunday morning didn't add up to fulfillment. Since we were unable to control our sexual desires, I begged him to go ahead and marry me right away, but he was unmovable in his determination to move ahead with his education first. Neither of us had told our families about how far the relationship had gone, and I was full of conflict. I had never had sex with anyone else before, and I only wanted to be with one person my whole life.

To complicate matters, one of his friends confided to me that my boyfriend had kissed another girl one night. Although he was remorseful when I confronted him, he still wasn't ready to "prove" he loved me by marrying me. Everything began to point to an ugly truth: I wasn't special enough to earn his love. IF he REALLY loved me, he'd marry me. IF he REALLY loved me, he wouldn't give in to the temptation of another girl. IF he REALLY loved me, he'd keep the alcohol away. IF he REALLY loved me . . . I began to fill in the blanks with many other truths that were staring me in the face. He DIDN'T "really" love me—not the way I needed to be loved.

I was heartbroken. I'd given him everything, but it had all been for nothing. The very thing I needed—what I thought he could give me—was unattainable after all. He didn't cherish me above everything else. I broke off our relationship, which was the hardest thing I'd ever done up to that point in my life. The awful truth was that even though I'd given all of myself I had to offer, it wasn't enough to make anyone love me the way I needed to be loved. I wasn't good enough.

The next few weeks and months were rough ones, but my mother, as always, was very helpful and supportive. I moved back home and finished the spring semester at school. Music helped me express all I was feeling. I sang out my anger with "You're So Vain (You probably think this song is about you!)," my heartache with "Pieces of April" (which my friend Fred had dedicated to me on the radio—sweet soothing to my pain as proof to the rest of Hutchinson that I was hurting!), and my depression with "Rainy Days and Mondays Always Get Me Down," along with many other tunes that summed up my misery.

Strangely enough, the heartbreak I experienced actually ended up being the best thing that could have happened to me. I realized in a small way that the only happiness I would ever find would come from a life that pleased God, letting Him fulfill me with the unconditional love I craved. A search began for this kind of relationship with God, and I found the Scriptures to be true, that if we seek Him with all of our hearts, He will be found. I called out to God from the depths of my being, saying that if He were real, I needed Him to make Himself real to me. He answered that prayer!

I had stopped going to my parents' church, but during this time of seeking, someone from that church called to invite me to a youth meeting. A lay witness mission was going on at church, and the youth were meeting in the home of a church member. That seemed non-threatening to me, so I agreed to go. Once there, I was pleasantly surprised by what I saw and heard. The music was lively, and the people were genuine. They shared testimonies of how the Lord had answered prayers and met their needs. He seemed so real to them, which was exactly what I was looking for.

Over the next few weeks and months, I spent as much time as possible with people from the lay witness missions all over Kansas, and I went back to church with my family. The Lord was drawing me, and I felt life was beginning to make sense for the first time. I finally came to the place where I knew I wanted to give all of myself to Him—the One Who really loved me—and He gave Himself to me, as well. I asked Him to completely fill me with His Spirit, and the intimacy I found with the Lord Jesus was beyond anything I'd ever dreamed. I spent several months of complete contentment and excitement as the Bible came alive to me, which drew me to read it during every spare moment. I found myself singing praises to Him instead of singing along with the pop songs that only accentuated and reinforced my pain. I began to heal.

As I grew in the Lord, I also prayed fervently for my family to know Him better. My mother had always had a deep faith that had carried her through the many hardships and heartaches she had borne, but I wanted *all* of the family to see Jesus the way I was seeing Him!

Since my relationship with Jesus was my entire focus, for my sophomore year, I transferred from our community college to Sterling College, a Presbyterian school in Sterling, Kansas. I thought that surely there I would get a strong grounding in God's Word, along with direction for what He wanted to do with my life. My lack of discipline pulled me down, though, and even though I loved the drama department, choir, and social life, I was oversleeping and missing classes, and my grades left much to be desired. I needed grounding in God's ways, and college wasn't the right setting for meeting that need in me.

The roots of dreams go deep, too, and there is a part of us that is created to seek a mate. I began to look for my earthly "prince" again, although this time I prayed for God's direction and will. Having already been sexually active, however, affected all my friendships with boys. It was all too easy to slip into sin, even when my intentions were good. The kind of man I wanted to marry—one who really loved the Lord and served Him—was quickly frightened away by my obvious eagerness to be more intimate physically than he wanted to be, since he wanted a godly relationship that was pleasing to the Lord. I had a few short relationships and thought I'd found love a couple of times, but deep down, I was mostly just yearning to somehow find a life that would please the Lord.

During this time, I heard about a Bible school called the Jesus Academy. It was about five miles south of Sterling, and I decided to visit it. My very first service there was amazing—it was like coming home! The praise and worship met a deep need in my heart to connect with the Lord. The preaching was the most relevant I'd ever experienced in my entire life. The other young people were appealing to me, because they shared my passion to know Jesus. I ended up dropping out of college at the end of the semester and moving to the Jesus Academy to live in the girls' "dorm," which was a trailer on the property.

Looking back, I have to chuckle at what must have been going through my parents' minds! With all the cults and weird stuff out there, naturally they were concerned about my well being. After all, I wasn't known for my level head! So they showed up at the school shortly after I moved in, and they were armed with lots of questions for the teachers! Thankfully, I was in good hands, and I continued to spend time with the family on the weekends; they even came out to some of our services from time to time.

I learned how to read my Bible and really understand what the Lord was saying to me through His Word. I learned how to share my faith. I made friends who are still some of the closest to my heart. It was a wonderful time of simply falling in love with Jesus more than ever.

Probably the most significant thing to happen in those first few months was that the Lord showed me I needed to forgive my father for the things he had done to hurt our family when I was growing up. I made the difficult decision to tell him that I was forgiving him, and I can still remember how important it was for both of us. He cried genuine tears of repentance and thanked me for releasing him in that way. It was a way to start fresh in our relationship, allowing us to build on the present love we shared instead of letting the past cast a shadow on everything between us. Daddy and I had always cared deeply for one another, but now we were developing a relationship full of trust and acceptance; he was becoming one of my best friends.

I did quickly become engaged to a young man at the Jesus Academy, but he had many challenges and wasn't ready for the kind of commitment marriage required. He had a habit of running away—literally leaving for days or weeks without a word. Before long, I broke up with him, thankful that the Lord had protected me from actually marrying him.

During this short, rocky engagement, I met a young man named Tracy Spencer. He was a new student at the Jesus Academy, arriving January 3rd, 1976, from Houston, Texas. I later learned that right from the start, Tracy noticed me and began to hope for a life together. Obviously, since I was engaged at the time, I wasn't looking, but even if I had been, Tracy just wasn't my "type." He enjoyed being outside involved in physical activities, while I was content inside reading a book or playing my guitar and singing. His background was far different from mine, too. Living in the city, Tracy had been addicted to drugs before he came to know Jesus' saving grace. I was from a small community in Kansas and had always shunned dating anyone involved with drugs. Our differences made Tracy a "safe" friend, and I considered him a great brother in the Lord.

A couple of months after my engagement was ended, Tracy and I ended up at the same prayer meeting. Tracy prayed aloud that the Lord would teach me to fear Him, which I thought was a strange request. After prayer, I told the group that I needed to get going, because I had to work the next morning. Tracy had slipped out without my noticing, so I was surprised when he came around the corner of the trailer and fell into step with me. He asked if I was going in to work the next morning, and I replied in the affirmative. I supposed he wanted me to pick up something for him in town. Imagine my surprise when he blurted out, "Well, I don't know how else to say it, but would you be my wife?"

I burst into laughter, thinking he was joking! It didn't take too long to realize that Tracy was NOT laughing! I was in total shock! You must realize that I was used to being wooed with flowers, dates, and special attention. I didn't even know Tracy *liked* me, much less that he was considering spending the rest of his life with me! There had never been a date or even sitting together at church or anything! True, he had managed to join me in a group of people when we attended Christian concerts or other activities, but I didn't ever catch on that he was only going along in order to be with me! I sobered up immediately then told him that I would have to think about it and pray! We parted ways, and in a state of total confusion, I visited one of our Bible teachers, Steve, to get his advice on what I should do.

I explained to Steve that I was confused because I had an inkling that yet *another* young man from the Jesus Academy was going to ask me to marry him. I hadn't dated this fellow, either, but I had at least noticed him paying attention to me. Any of you who have attended Bible college might be able to identify with the group of people who believe that falling in love has very little to do with choosing a mate! I, along with most of my classmates, believed that the Lord had someone picked out for me, and that the marriage would be obedience to God rather than the kind of love that the world offered. After all, I didn't have a very good track record of my own, and I didn't want to make a mistake when it came to actually walking down the aisle.

Well, my teacher was not of that school! When I explained the situation with both young men, he asked me which one I loved! I wasn't in love with either one of them! I can't even remember what other advice I was given because it was foreign to my new way of thinking, but I knew I had to have an answer from the Lord.

The next evening before church started, Tracy passed me in the hall and didn't even look at me, much less act as if he wanted to marry me! All through the service, I thought about him and wondered what in the world was going on. When church was over, I approached Tracy and asked him if we could talk. I explained to him that if he were serious about wanting to marry me, he would need to spend some time with me so I could get to know him and make an informed decision. He helped me understand his hesitance; he had been engaged before, but the girl had broken off their plans. This caused Tracy to fear rejection, so he didn't want to influence me in any way. Although he truly loved me and knew he wanted to marry me, he also didn't want to pursue a relationship that wasn't God's plan for him. He didn't want to be hurt again. We agreed that we would spend some time together to see where our relationship would go, and I invited him to come with me to my parents' home the following afternoon. I knew Mama wouldn't mind one extra mouth to feed!

Tracy walked me back to my trailer and kissed me good night. I knew then that he was serious about marriage, because in our circle of friends, that was almost as good as a commitment!

In all the years I'd dated, my father and I had never really agreed on the type of guy I should have a relationship with. He distrusted most of the guys I liked. I resented what I considered his interference, yet I have to admit that he often had the fellows pegged pretty well. When I took Tracy home for the first time, on Father's Day, 1976, he and Dad really hit it off. They spent most of the afternoon sitting in the back yard sharing their testimonies of how they had come to know Jesus and what He'd done in their lives. It was refreshing to me; I didn't feel I had to impress anyone or convince my family of anything—after all, I wasn't even sure myself where our friendship would go. I relaxed, happy that at least Daddy and I both *liked* Tracy. It was a starting place.

I don't remember much about Monday, but the Tuesday after Tracy's proposal stands out in my memory, because the events of the evening changed the course of my life. We were eating spaghetti in the cafeteria at the Jesus Academy, visiting with an older friend. It's funny that I can remember exactly what we were eating, yet I can't recall any of that conversation; another Voice seemed to be speaking to me, calling for my complete attention. During our meal, I believed I heard the Holy Spirit saying, "In your marriage to this man, I will teach you how to die to your flesh."

My first thought was, "Now, *that's* romantic!" Flashing back to the kind of dating I was used to in my past (complete with flowers, candy, movies, going out to eat, etc.), dying to my flesh did NOT sound like a viable option! However, taking into account the new mindset I had taken on at the Jesus Academy, it makes sense that I would respond to that type of message from the Lord. It fit my new ideas of what marriage would be. I told Tracy later that evening that I would marry him. We had known each other for six and a half months, and we set the wedding date for only three months later.

In the years since then, I've wondered whether or not it was really the Lord speaking to me or just my own thinking. Really, it doesn't matter! Maybe He was giving me direction; I'd asked Him to do so, and John 10 tells us that His sheep hear His voice. Maybe He just knew that I was going to say yes, so He was letting me know what it would be like; of course, ALL marriages do the same work in us if we allow them to! Maybe it was my own thinking, as I suggested; the point is, I took it seriously and made a commitment to Tracy, so the "why's" and "supposed to's" and all the rest really don't make any difference! Once we said our "I do's," the reasons for them no longer carried any bearing on the commitment.

The Lord gave Tracy a Scripture for our marriage; it's found in Colossians 1:17b, and reads, "By [Jesus] all things hold together." Somehow Tracy knew that only the Lord could keep us together, so we had that verse printed on our napkins for the wedding reception. Little did I know how true those words would be for us as the trials of life came.

I wish I could say that the engagement was sweet and that our love grew, but it wasn't like that for me. Tracy really did seem to love me, but I had no romantic feelings towards him at all. We worked during the day and went to classes at the Jesus Academy Monday through Wednesday nights. Thursday nights were prayer meeting and Bible study, and Friday nights were used for outreach into the community. We had church on Saturday nights and Sunday mornings, so there wasn't a lot of time for us to get to know each other in the light of our new commitment to one another. The little bit of time we spent alone together usually ended up being more intimate physically than I wanted, and it was just a matter of time before we actually had intercourse. I began to feel trapped in the relationship. Since we had not stayed pure sexually, I felt I had no choice but to marry Tracy. In my thinking, it was better to just marry him and be done with the cycle of failure; I didn't want to give myself to yet another man who didn't commit to me. He was ready and waiting to marry me, so I agreed.

The Scripture tells us, "You can be sure your sin will find you out." That is exactly what happened to us! We found a house to rent in Sterling, and I went ahead and moved into it so we wouldn't be paying double for my accommodations during the month and a half before the wedding. Tracy spent the night with me one night, and someone saw his car and called the school! The teachers called us into the office and asked us if we were having sex with each other. Although I was embarrassed—mortified—I was also relieved to be called into accountability. I readily admitted our sin, glad to have it out in the open. Tracy was hesitant and didn't want to admit it, which irritated and angered me. Our teachers made it clear that we had to stop or we would be expelled. They prayed with us and encouraged us, and we got through that last month before the wedding without giving in to temptation.

So on September 18, 1976, I walked down the aisle to marry Tracy Spencer. Even when it was time for my dad to lead me in, I was panicked, wondering if I was doing the right thing. I prayed fervently, "Lord, if this isn't right, please stop me!" It was a far cry from what I'd dreamed of all my life, and nothing about our situation resembled the fairytale romance I'd grown up with. But no heavenly intervention took place, so we took our vows.

The actual wedding was nice; we have my mother to thank for that. I had dreamed of a hippie style of wedding. Not that I was really a hippie, mind you, but I was a hippie "wannabe." I thought that since I wore blue jeans and T-shirts, preferred bare feet to shoes, played "Rocky Mountain High" on my guitar, and used Herbal Essence shampoo, that qualified me! I wanted to be married outside in a long hippie dress, Tracy in jeans, both of us barefoot, guitar music playing, and flowers in my hair. Mama talked me into trying on traditional wedding gowns, though, and when she broke into tears seeing me in one of them, I gave in. If I had been more aware of my own feelings, I would have realized why I was willing to let her have the wedding the way she wanted it; I couldn't see that it was because I wasn't really into the marriage, so the wedding itself wasn't as important to me as it should have been.

After our wedding ceremony, one of our teachers, Jack Park, came through the receiving line and told us, "It's okay now." I knew what he meant and was thankful that he was giving us his blessing, letting us know that we didn't have to live with the guilt of our previous sin. But we really didn't understand the consequences that sexual sin would bring into our marriage. We hoped that being married would take care of the issue, but we were learning that the wages of sin is death, even after we are Christians. It affected the way we looked at each other. I disrespected Tracy for not being a stronger leader in our relationship—for pressuring me to do something I knew was wrong. I felt unloved, too—not cherished as special. Even though we knew Jesus had to be the foundation of our life together, we had built on the foundation with something shaky, and it caused problems for years.

Mama had bought Tracy and me matching outfits to wear as we left the church. Rice in our hair, we ran to our car with cameras flashing. We didn't leave for our honeymoon yet, though; we went to my parents' house to open our gifts so Tracy's folks could see them. I didn't even think it was strange that I was in no hurry to leave with my new husband. Since we'd already had sex, there was no need to rush off to share that marital joy. There was no comprehension of leaving father and mother and cleaving to my new spouse.

In fact, there was very little understanding of any other principles of marriage. We had received very little premarital counseling. The pastor of my parents' church met with us once or twice, and all we can remember from that is his asking us a hypothetical question: If we were alone on a stranded island, would we still feel it necessary to get married, or would we just "live together"? We thought it was ridiculous—and still think so today! That was the extent of our preparation for marriage, besides watching our own parents for nineteen years.

But we were off to start our "happily ever after." The royal theme of Prince Charming had even played out in our music at the wedding. We had asked a friend to sing "Let Us Climb the Hill Together," and one line from the song is, "I will make you queen of my home under the glory of the King; we'll raise our family in a castle full of love and trust the Lord in everything." My prince's crown was somewhat tarnished and askew, and I was *not* feeling like a queen. But being an optimist, I believed that with the Lord on our side, His love would conquer all, and we would find marital bliss. Boy, did I have a surprise coming!

2. The Wonderful Kingdom of Shackri-La!

It's true that somewhere in la-la land there exists a place called Shangri-La. It is actually a fictional, peaceful Tibetan mountain retreat where no one grows old, found in James Hilton's *Lost Horizon.* I had always pictured it as a wondrous place of beauty where love could grow and be nurtured, much like my white-picket fence vision of years gone by.

Well, Tracy and I spent our honeymoon in a cabin in Evergreen, Colorado, just outside of Denver. The name posted on the cabin was "Shackri-La!" How fitting for the type of week we ended up having.

We went to this cabin because our close friend, Geoff D'Urso, had a cousin who owned it and was willing to let us stay for free! We only took a honeymoon because my parents gave us $100 as a wedding gift. I had expected the rustic environment of the Rocky Mountains to be the perfect start to our marriage, Tracy chopping wood for the fire, my serenading him with my guitar, away from phones and bills and distractions. I envisioned romantic evenings snuggled up close to the man I had committed my life to.

Neither of us took into account the fact that we knew nothing about braving the wilds of Colorado! Tracy was a city-boy from Houston, and I was a Kansas girl who hadn't been to the mountains since childhood! We had no experience in what it would take to make our time together a successful first week of marriage! And that was just considering the physical tasks that would be necessary, not the emotional or spiritual demands that learning to live with another person would entail!

When we first arrived, we eagerly began unloading our car. We brought our typical hippie attire of jeans, overalls, and T-shirts with our flip-flop sandals and tennis shoes. Thankfully, we had thrown in a couple of jackets. We planned to cook most of our own meals to save money, so we were ready to get everything unpacked and put away.

We had quite a surprise waiting for us because Geoff's cousin had forgotten to tell the neighbors in the nearby cabin that we were coming up for the week. Since they had no idea other human beings would be in the area, they hadn't penned up their Irish wolfhounds! We had taken one load into the house and had come out for the next one, when we heard a guttural growl that made the hairs on our arms and heads stand straight up. Glancing up slowly, we saw four beasts with bared teeth, ready to take us on for invading their space! They were relatively quiet compared to the tiny Chihuahua that was yipping loudly in protest of our arrival! We didn't know what to do, and although we knew very little about dogs, we were still fairly certain we were in deep trouble! We instinctively moved very slowly and began to pray fervently for our lives! These dogs were not kidding about protecting their turf! Tracy managed to get a snapshot of them before they mysteriously began to turn one by one and go back to their own yard. The little dog was the last to go! I was furious with Tracy for thinking it was funny to take the picture instead of trying to save me! Already I was starting to suspect that he wasn't cut out for knighthood or rescuing me, his damsel in distress. I began to have a niggling thought in the back of my mind: he must not really care about me like I needed him to!

Of course, we had no experience with lighting a wood-burning stove! I was putting our belongings away while Tracy tried to get a fire going before the temperature outside dipped too low. He managed to get a rip-roaring flame started up, but before we knew what had gone wrong, the entire cabin was filled with smoke! I had mascara streaming down my face as my eyes watered, and he was opening windows and doors before trying to get the contraption to quit belching more smoke into the atmosphere!

We finally cleared the smoke, cleaned up the mess, and came up with something to eat. Although there was no running water, which I found tremendously romantic, there *was* electricity AND a television in the bedroom.

That would have been fine, except that our first evening there, Tracy decided to watch "Charlie's Angels." I don't know how much you know about the program, but it was a detective series about three beautiful women who were undercover agents fighting crime. It was an entertaining show, but being a newly married, insecure young lady of only nineteen, I really didn't care to compete with three gorgeous women in my honeymoon bedroom! So I demanded that he turn it off, acting affronted that he would even consider it a viable option to watch in the first place. I was wounded, touchy, and indignant!

Poor Tracy didn't have much of a chance! He was doomed no matter what he did! If he gave in to me and turned off the television, it would seem like he had no backbone and that he would spend our married life bending to my every whim. If he went ahead and watched the show instead of backing down at my request, he would appear unconcerned with my feelings. Since he really couldn't even begin to understand what my problem was in the first place, and his own desire to be the leader and man of the house was running strong, he opted to keep the show on. The poor man had no clue what the results of his decision would be!

I sulked and pouted and cried for the entire program. Since my ranting and raving hadn't done any good, I gave him the silent treatment after the program. I was inconsolable, even when he tried to talk to me. Finally in desperation, he told me he was just going to sit in the next room and read his Bible. "Sure," I thought, "Mr. Spiritual! You can treat me like dirt, but then read your Bible and think that will make everything all okay. Some kind of leader! If you were any kind of Christian man, you would take care of my needs before your own. You are nothing more than a pervert, anyway, wanting to watch those flashy girls on television! How dare you want to look at them when you have a new wife here, waiting to be with you! You don't care about me at all! Well, just don't think I'm going to let you get close to me now that you've hurt me like this! I won't forgive you after hurting me so deeply . . . " And on and on it went, a continual torrent in my mind, accusing Tracy of things he had never held in his heart. I couldn't see that he was caught between his desire to love me, and his need to be respected as a man. I didn't know anything about putting his needs ahead of my own; in fact, I was so self-centered that I didn't even consider the possibility that he had needs I wasn't automatically meeting simply by gracing his life with my presence! Neither of us realized patterns were being set that would take us years to overcome.

After a while, I needed to go to the bathroom, and since there was no running water, the only option was to make a trek to the outhouse. By then it was dark outside, and anyone who has stayed on a Colorado mountain knows that dark up there is not like the dark of the Kansas prairies! It was pitch black, and there were enough undefined noises to make even a grown man take notice! Besides, after our run-in with the Irish wolfhounds, I was somewhat tentative about what I might meet out there in the dark!

Thinking I would really show Tracy how badly he had hurt me, though, and desiring to fully communicate to him that I could do just fine without him, I put on my shoes and started for the door. He asked me where I was going, and I self-righteously replied that I needed to go to the bathroom. Mentally, I was picturing the Irish wolfhounds again, along with bears and deer and bobcats—and who knew what other critters could be waiting for me once I stepped out the door. I figured it would just teach Tracy a much-needed lesson if something ate me alive! Then he'd be sorry for how he'd acted!

He asked me to wait just a minute while he put on his shoes to walk me out. I sassed back that I didn't need his help, then moved to go on out. He repeated his intent to escort me; I retorted forcefully that I was going without him. I could sense he was beginning to get a little irritated with me as we went back and forth on the issue. Finally, he took me by surprise by physically picking me up, tossing me back onto the bed, and *commanding* me to wait there while he put his shoes on so he could walk me out!

I was in total shock! Nobody had ever treated me like that before in my life! Not that my parents didn't make me mind, because they did. I'd had my share of spankings and discipline as a child. Still, I had also learned to manipulate most people into giving me my own way. But now my tears and pouting and stubbornness had not produced the desired result—to make Tracy regret ever crossing me!

I want to be sure to communicate that there was nothing abusive in Tracy's actions or attitude or heart. He didn't hurt me, nor did he make me feel threatened physically. There was no indication that he would use physical pain to bend me to his will then or ever. It wasn't that kind of scenario at all! Instead, it was just his only way of getting me to shut my mouth long enough to realize that he was not going to give in to me on every little thing, but that didn't mean he didn't love me or desire to protect me. He simply would not allow me to put myself in harm's way just because I was too stubborn to listen to him!

Once the shock wore off, which took all the rest of the evening, an unconscious battle had begun: who was going to lead our family? Or more specifically, who was going to lead me? I was strong-willed and opinionated, full of my own convictions about what was right and wrong. I had never really let another person tell me how life would be for me. Even in kindergarten, my teacher had told my mother how good I was at making decisions! I knew what I wanted, or so I thought, and had a pretty well-defined plan for how I'd get it! Receiving attention was way up at the top of my list! Tracy was also stubborn, if not as strong-willed, and he was not going to relinquish his own ideas of what was right and good without a fight! Although neither of us realized it or understood it, the next few years would be a painful continuation of our struggle to see who would come out on top in the battle of the wills.

Shackri-La. . . not only the name of our honeymoon spot, but a foreshadowing of the truth that our reality was destined to fail to live up to our dreams.

3. Queen Jezebel

Jezebel was King Ahab's wife, and she is introduced in the Bible in I Kings 16. Her husband Ahab did more evil in the eyes of the Lord and provoked God more than any of the Israelite kings before him. He looked lightly upon his sin, and marrying Jezebel was just one in the long list of wrongs he committed. She was the daughter of Ethbaal, king of the Sidonians, and not an Israelite woman, so Ahab should never have looked twice at this foreign woman. God knew that the Israelites would be drawn to false gods if they intermarried with the foreign women, so He forbade it. But Ahab had no consideration for God or His laws, even though he was the king and his actions affected so many other people.

This couple made quite a pair. I Kings 21:25-26 says this about the two of them: "There was never a man like Ahab, who sold himself to do evil in the eyes of the Lord, urged on by Jezebel his wife. He behaved in the vilest manner by going after idols, like the Amorites the Lord drove out before Israel."

Jezebel's name means "without cohabitation, unhusbanded, unexalted." True to her name, Jezebel was a rebellious woman, not willing to be under any man—not even her husband, who was also her king. She did as she pleased and lived as though she was not married. Ethbaal, her father's name, means "with Baal" or "Baal's man." Baal was the primary false god that the people of the land of Canaan worshipped, and his name means "master" or "possessor." When we read about Baal worship in the Bible, we find that it is always tied in with sexual worship. Ashtoroth is the female counterpart god that was worshipped in Canaan. The word Sidon, which was where Jezebel was from, means "fortified." The false gods that ruled her land had built up or fortified a strong unseen kingdom.

Today we might think that worshipping false gods is ancient or foreign, but actually these false gods represented demon spirits that Satan has used for centuries to lead people astray. Perhaps looking at the functions of these two gods will help bring it into language that will help us understand how it affects our American society. When a man and woman are being influenced by the same evil spirits that Baal and Ashtoroth represented, we find that he worships her for sex, while she worships him for security. Worship doesn't always mean bowing your head down to the ground and waving your arms up and down! It can mean living like the object of your worship is worthy of everything you can offer. It can be putting that person before everyone and everything else. When it applies to another human being, it might mean ignoring your own conscience in order to please that person or even endangering yourself for him or her. In light of those definitions, we all know people who have fallen into this trap that the devil has used for years to hurt us and keep us from knowing the Lord intimately.

Four hundred fifty prophets of Baal ate at Jezebel's table, and she slew all the true prophets of God that she could. In fact, human life meant nothing to her. In I Kings 21, we read that one day Ahab was pouting, and she asked him why. She discovered that he had been unable to purchase a certain vineyard from a man named Naboth. It had belonged to Naboth's family, and he didn't want to lose it. Ahab was so upset about it that he wouldn't even eat. Jezebel told him to cheer up and eat, because she would get the vineyard for him. She sent letters with Ahab's seal on them to the officials of the city, calling for a day of fasting. Naboth was to be seated in a prominent place, but two scoundrels were to be seated across from him in order to falsely accuse him of cursing God and Ahab. Her plan was to then have him stoned. Her orders were carried out, and after Naboth's death, Ahab went down to take possession of the vineyard. Jezebel didn't care about the vineyard, but she loved the power she had over others, particularly over men. She expected to have anything she wanted, and she wouldn't see her husband deprived of anything he wanted, either.

Jezebel's name is mentioned again in the Bible in the book of Revelation. There she's portrayed as a woman who uses her sensuality to appear spiritual; she claims to have God's Word, but she is filled with deception. She hasn't got a "covering;" she's husbandless in the sense of being rebellious and not willing to submit. Men follow her because of the demonic anointing she has and her promiscuity.

Certainly, as a Christian woman who loved the Lord, there would be no correlation between wicked Jezebel and me, right? Wrong! I had some of the same seeds of rebellion sown in my own human nature, and in those early years of marriage, they brought forth fruit that was destructive to our marriage.

Despite my fantasy of the white picket fence, birds and butterflies flitting nearby, and cheery, chubby children laughing and frolicking in the yard, I spent the first few years of married life in strife. Tracy and I argued about almost everything. We bickered about little things like where we should eat out or how to properly dispense toothpaste and toilet paper. We disagreed on more important topics such as how to discipline our children or what church we should attend. We were growing in the Lord as individuals, yet the fussing with each other never stopped for long.

We even fought about our faith. When Tracy felt ill, he would give a good confession that he was healed, and I would go ballistic on him! I would point out the obvious facts: he had a cough, a fever, and green stuff blowing out of his nose! I argued that if that was healing, I didn't think God would want credit for it! I insisted that it was fine to ask God to heal him and to even have faith that He would, but it went totally against my better sense to say it had already happened when everything we could see said otherwise.

I had no idea how much I was crushing Tracy and the belief system he had developed over time. I was just SO strong in personality and debating that eventually he gave up the fight. He was beaten, yet there were no winners. The victory was not sweet and I was never satisfied. I continually looked for something else to attack. I couldn't see past my own opinions in order to consider his ideas as possibilities for growth in my own spiritual walk with God.

I also crushed his attempts to show me love. When he first met me, Tracy was smitten immediately. He says that it was the sweet, gentle spirit he saw and the light in my eyes that drew him, but living with me was an entirely different story. I was hard, selfish, and insistent on my own way. I not only had to have our plans go my way, but I also had to be right about everything. There was no compromising with me; it was all or nothing, and I was never satisfied.

At first, my husband tried to show me his love through the gifts he brought to me. Even in this area, I cut him down. I was so picky that nothing he gave me was good enough. I'm embarrassed and ashamed to remember it now, but during that first year of marriage, he bought me a negligee that had caught his attention because the decoration on the front looked like an "S." Since our last name was Spencer, he thought that was pretty neat. I thought it was ridiculous and let him know so! I couldn't imagine choosing a nightie based on something so juvenile! Instead of taking pride in bearing his name, I was rejecting Tracy's efforts to bless me. I preferred that he simply give me the money to purchase my own presents so I could choose exactly what I wanted!

Years later, when he didn't buy me anything for Mother's Day or my birthday or Christmas, I was hurt and offended, never realizing it was my own fault. The poor man couldn't do anything right in my eyes, so he simply quit trying. He just went along with me to get along.

Please realize that even though I'm shining the spotlight on insecurity that my husband suffered from, it doesn't mean that macho men are healthy! They also deal with insecurities, but they live them out by bullying others instead of by giving up.

Eventually Tracy quit trying to lead our home, too. He tells me that he knows exactly when he completely gave up, but the process leading to that time was gradual and painful. The very thing I really wanted, I tore down with my own hands, especially with my words. I am amazed that Tracy even stayed with me, because I was giving nothing into the relationship to meet his needs. I was impossible to please and hard to live with.

My vow that I would never let a man treat me the way my dad treated my mom was the result of fear. In an effort to protect myself, *I* ended up being the one who gave Tracy twenty questions if he came home five minutes late! *I* was the critical, suspicious, controlling one. I became what I vowed I'd never take from someone else.

We eventually found a way to live together in relative peace, although there was no satisfaction in our relationship. He continued to love me and put up with me, while I found meaning through raising our children, trying to be the perfect mother. As long as he didn't interfere with that, we usually managed to live civilly.

Jezebel's sins were rebellion, spiritual pride, and sexual sin—she wanted to be worshipped, and she wanted to be in control. I thought that since I had given up my promiscuous past for a walk with Jesus, then I was nothing like her, not realizing how much she and I had in common. Thankfully, the Lord is full of grace and mercy; He loves us as we are but also loves us enough not to leave us there! Ultimately, I really wanted to worship Him and have my character changed to be like Him, and He was willing to prove Himself faithful in that area. But I learned that when pride is involved, sometimes things have to get pretty bad before we're willing to see ourselves honestly. That lesson was around the corner for me when we'd been married for about ten years.

4. Camelot

Nothing about our marriage was like the peaceful Camelot, except for the entrance of a trusted male friend who ended up stealing the queen's heart. That is exactly what happened with us. While living in another state, Tracy and I had a friend whom I will call Gene. He was just a couple of years younger than we were, and he had never married. Gene was a musician and songwriter, so he and I shared many of the same interests and characteristics. We worked together on some projects at our church, including being on the praise team and co-writing and directing some major musical productions. He spent lots of time with our family, and even lived with us for a few months while we were discipling some of the young adults.

I had told Tracy at one time that I felt attracted to Gene, and I even asked Tracy not to go on to bed in the evenings when Gene was visiting us. I felt it was inappropriate to be alone with him while everyone else was sleeping. Tracy didn't seem to be worried about it, though, so he would still head to bed when he got tired. Even though I didn't think it looked good for me to be alone with Gene, I still felt I was strong enough to withstand temptation. My beliefs about adultery were set in stone, and I had no tolerance for others who had fallen; I certainly didn't really believe I was at risk! I believed I was as devoted to the Lord as possible, and I didn't want to do anything to hurt my relationship with Him. Besides, Gene was a dear friend to both Tracy and me, and he was a sincere Christian who wanted to walk with the Lord in a deeper way, too. So I felt we were actually quite safe, regardless of appearances.

When the time came for us to move back to Kansas, Tracy left early to start his job while I stayed behind to let the children finish the last three weeks of school. During this time Gene was helping me with a recording project, so we were spending lots of time together in Tracy's absence. I enjoyed his company and it seemed he met many of my needs for attention and conversation. He was a great listener and capable of communicating his own feelings effectively, as well. I should have realized how close to danger I was getting when he confessed that he was attracted to me. I should have run as fast as I could! But I was hungry for someone to pay attention to me, and my loneliness was speaking much more loudly than my common sense. I told him that I had also been attracted to him. The feelings that were sparked from speaking these words were major red flags, but I ignored them. We enjoyed our last few days together, taking care not to become physically involved, yet longing to see more of each other. It was hard to move away from him, yet I did so with his promise that he would come to see us soon.

The children and I joined Tracy in Kansas in June, and I stayed in touch with Gene, finally getting his commitment to visit us in July. Interestingly enough, even though before this I had always let Tracy know when I was being tempted by an attraction to another man, I wasn't telling him this time how my attraction to Gene had grown. I had moved into a new stage: I didn't want Tracy to protect me from anything happening. I wasn't consciously aware that I was looking for an intimate relationship with Gene, yet inside it was exactly what I was longing for. He had seemed to meet so many of my needs that I didn't want to let go of the chance to experience more of the same.

I watched what I ate so I wouldn't gain any weight before Gene came, and I tried to get a little tan. I spent hours in front of the mirror, arranging my hair in different styles and applying my makeup carefully to achieve just the right look. The day of Gene's arrival was quickly approaching, and I wanted to be at my best.

He came with an indefinite plan of when he would leave. We spent wonderful days together while Tracy was at work. We sang, wrote music, laughed, and shared hearts. He helped around the house and talked to me or played the piano while I cooked. He played with the children and went to church with us. I was leading worship at our church already, and he taught me many new worships songs I could use with our worship team. He stood in the hall and watched me apply my makeup, telling me how cute I was in the way I contorted my face just so to do my mascara and lipstick. We checked out records at the library and played classical music while we waltzed around my kitchen. It was all still just a flirtatious game to me, and I didn't foresee how very dangerous it was becoming. Even when we began to touch hands briefly, I still didn't want to see where it was headed, because I didn't want it to end.

The real trouble started one night while he and I were folding clothes after everyone else had already gone to bed. We had been laughing and sharing, when suddenly Gene reached over and took my hand and gazed in to my eyes, tenderly telling me he loved me. I know my response startled him, because I yanked my hand away and began to cry. He wanted to know what was wrong, naturally being confused because my actions up to that point had led him to believe I wanted a relationship with him as much as he wanted one with me. But to me, after being married for ten years, saying the words, "I love you," involved commitment! In my mind, you didn't tell someone you loved her without expecting a long-term relationship with her! If he hadn't voiced the words, I could have just kept pretending, fantasizing that we could have something that wouldn't really change my entire life or hurt anybody else. But to actually put words to the feelings moved our situation from playing make-believe to facing the reality of what I was doing. I DID feel that I loved him and finally told him so, but instead of making me happy, it only made me more miserable than I'd been. It meant I had to make a decision about what to do with my feelings.

He asked me how I felt about my relationship with the Lord, and I wasn't sure how to respond. I was confused, because I had given all of myself I could give to the Lord. I had trusted the Lord to meet my needs, and for years I'd thrown myself into Bible study and ministry to those He sent my way. I began to think that perhaps I had used "religion" to fill the void caused by my unhappy marriage. That was just another lie the enemy of our souls was using to add confusion. The truth was, I was using my relationship with Gene to fill a void only the Lord CAN fill!

The next few days were a combination of ecstasy and agony. We held one another and expressed our love through words and looks and touching during the day when the children were napping and late at night when everyone was asleep again. We carefully watched our actions when the family was together. We discussed what we should do, and he begged me to leave with him, bringing the children along to go back to his home and be with him. I was torn, knowing that I loved him, believing I could never have that kind of intimacy with Tracy, and yet fearing God. I was, after all, not merely a nominal Christian, but someone who had given my entire life to Jesus in service and love. I also knew what His Word said about the consequences of adultery.

I argued with God and tried to bargain with Him. I was angry with Him, believing He had led me to marry someone who would never be able to meet my needs, yet putting me in the position of having to say goodbye to what I thought was true love—if I wanted to continue to please God and live for Him. I reminded the Lord about David and Bathsheba—after all, they ended up being together even though their beginning was sin! Of course, the Holy Spirit was quick to remind me that their oldest son also died because of their sin! (2 Samuel 11 & 12)

I fantasized about what it would be like to actually be married to Gene, although the word "marriage" had never come up. That meant I had to get rid of Tracy in my mind, and I wished him dead. If Tracy died, I would be free in God's eyes to be with the one I loved. Even in the middle of the sin and betrayal, I still wanted to do what was right, and I was desperately trying to find a way to make my love for Gene right.

It was a no-win situation; I would have to either disobey God and leave my husband, uprooting my children and turning their lives upside down, or I'd have to give up the one man I'd ever known who seemed to fit perfectly with what I needed and wanted in a relationship. The days and nights were spent in bittersweet reflection and wavering as the war inside me raged. When I read my Bible and prayed, I could sense the Lord saying He understood what I was going through and cared deeply, but right was still right and wrong was still wrong.

Finally, at the close of his third week with us, I knew I had to ask Gene to leave. It wasn't that I cared about what my sin would do to Tracy or the children, nor was it a noble decision to do what was right; in fact, it was simply the fear of God that kept me from going ahead and having an affair with this man. I knew that because the Lord had given me so much from His Word and had loved me deeply, then much was also required of me. I had a sense that there was a line I simply could not cross or the consequences would be unbearable. Still, the decision to ask him to leave also seemed impossible to bear.

Two things have stood out in my memory of those last few hours before Gene left and the hours immediately following. First, he and I sat on the sofa to say our goodbyes, and I sarcastically commented that Tracy and I would probably end up leading marriage seminars someday! (Who knew that in years to come God would actually use my relationship with Tracy to minister to other couples!) The second is that the day Gene left, my husband came home from work that evening with a single-stemmed rose for me. He was not the kind of man to give flowers or anything else remotely romantic! And his intention was not to actually romance me, but rather to comfort me. He wanted me to know that he knew I was hurting and to let me know he cared.

I have asked Tracy if he realized what was happening while Gene was visiting, and he says he didn't. But I believe that deep down, he had to know. Why else would he have brought the rose? He was very tender and quiet for the next few days. There had to be something in his spirit that was speaking to him, but the day for actually revealing the truth to him in a more obvious way was to come much later. For the time being, he was just giving me room to grieve.

I cried for days. My heart felt like it was being ripped from my chest, and I was inconsolable. I shared with a couple of close friends and my mother and one of my sisters, knowing confession was good for the soul, yet I was hurting beyond belief. Gene was gone, and I was just trying to cope with living without him.

I continued to read my Bible each morning, but I was full of anger and beginning to be bitter. I would tell the Lord each day that I was going to read His Word, but I didn't know why! After all, I didn't believe He would speak to me, and even if He did, I wouldn't believe Him because I believed He had lied to me. I felt that He had let me down, that the Christian life was supposed to be full of love and goodness and happiness, yet I'd been miserable in marriage for ten years and had no hope of anything ever changing. I had sacrificed true love for the Lord, and in my mind, it was a bad bargain! I didn't see anything I was going to gain from it, except perhaps to avoid judgment. Even that was questionable. Although this man and I hadn't had sex, our intimacy had gone further than it should have. I should never have even touched him or held him or kissed him. And my heart had been totally unfaithful, so I feared the consequences for that would fall unexpectedly in spite of my decision to be obedient to God's Word. I thought I might have a car accident or a heart attack or be struck by lightning. It was incomprehensible to me that God would forgive me or ever use me in ministry again. It was the darkest time of my life.

I felt I needed to do something to fill my time, and a Christian education for my children was very important to me. I ended up home-schooling Sara for third grade, and I also started a day care center in my home. I also re-enrolled in Sterling College, glad to learn that my theatre scholarship would be renewed. I decided to get my degree in elementary education, mostly because if the state of Kansas ever made it difficult for home-schoolers, I would have my certificate from the state and avoid trouble. It helped me to have my time filled so completely.

Meanwhile, the Lord was gently letting me know He was not angry with me. Day after day He did speak to me, despite my angry accusations that He would not. He let me know in many different ways that He loved me, even though I was not responsive to His love at that time. I was reading about the Lord delivering His people from the bondage and slavery of Egypt, and He was showing me how it applied to my situation. While writing this book, I looked back over some of the journal entries I had written during the first month after Gene left, and I was encouraged to see how His Word had helped me get through it.

August 1, 1986 Exodus 3:21-22 says, "And I will make the Egyptians favorably disposed toward this people, so that when you leave you will not go empty-handed. Every woman is to ask her neighbor for articles of silver and gold and for clothing, which you will put on your sons and daughters. And so you will plunder the Egyptians." Even the things that bind me and have me in slavery will not triumph over me. I'm going to milk them for all they're worth! I'm going to take ALL the good with me out of this experience—on my way out of bondage into freedom!

Later that day I wrote that I knew the Lord was my provider. At church before he left, Gene had sung "All I have needed Thy hand hath provided! Great is Thy faithfulness, Lord, unto me." God was saying that even when I was faithless, He remained faithful.

August 6, 1986 In Exodus 4, Moses makes excuses to God about why he isn't a good candidate for what God wants him to do. The Lord moves miraculously to show Moses He is the One who will free His people. I feel like I'm saying, "Lord, what if I can't do it?" And He's saying that He's able—He'll provide even the miraculous if that's what it takes. I should believe Him and be willing instead of insisting He do it my way.

August 11, 1986 In Exodus 5 - 12, after God said He was going to free His people through Moses, they first see their workload doubled and their lives harder. God says what He's going to do and it looks like the opposite happens! In fact, it gets worse! Instead of being released, the Israelites' bondage grew more severe!

n my life, God has spoken to me that He is my Provider and He WILL meet my needs (emotional in this case). I will NOT look at my circumstances to see if He's keeping His Word! I will just believe Him and wait on Him. He knows me better than anyone else does, thus knowing my needs better than I do! I will wait on the Lord and let Him do it His way; proving that ***He is the Lord!***

I read about Pharoah's sorcerers somehow making their staffs turn into snakes, just as Aaron's staff had become a snake. But Aaron's staff swallowed up their staffs! The Lord showed me that there can be a counterfeit for what He wants to do. But when He really "gets down to business," the enemy can't even mimic the real thing anymore! He wanted me to see that Gene was just a counterfeit for the real thing He longed to give me.

August 12, 1986 Exodus 13:17-18 "When Pharoah let the people go, God did not lead them on the road through the Philistine country, though that was shorter. For God said, 'If they face war, they might change their minds and return to Egypt.' So God led the people around by the desert road toward the Red Sea. The Israelites went up out of Egypt armed for battle." Sometimes I'd rather go back into bondage than to fight! In that case, He takes me through a dry land—a desert—to get to my destination or to buy time till I'm ready to face my foes. In my situation right now, it's time to rise up and fight—meet the enemy head-on! I don't have time to waste on a wilderness journey—there are people all around me who need Jesus—AND I have a family here that needs a wife and mother able to function and minister to their needs.

August 14, 1986 In Exodus 16, the Israelites griped about being hungry and reminisced about the meat and other food they had in Egypt. So the Lord sent them quail and manna to eat. Ah, grumbling! When will I learn? The Lord plans GOOD for me—I should rest in Him and trust Him instead of complaining. They could have been enjoying their lives and His guidance instead of misusing precious time by griping. PLEASE, Lord, teach me to trust and enjoy this life You've provided.

I think sometimes His provision is right under my nose or within my reach, but I miss it because I'm complaining and magnifying little problems.

August 15, 1986 Moses had a staff in his hand when God called him—what do I have? I have all the right "ingredients" to be a "good" wife—cooking, cleaning, loving, caring, seeing joy in little things, talents, etc. I can expect God to use what I've already got—AND the ***man*** *I've already got!*

I read in Exodus 17:8-15 about Moses holding up his hands while the Israelites fought the Amalekites. As long as his hands were up, the Israelites won, but if he grew weary and let his hands down, the Israelites began to lose. Aaron and Hur helped Moses keep his hands up. God was showing me that as long as I was calling out on Him, I'd have victory. When I grew weary, I would need my friends to hold me up. I realized that when I was having trouble, I could call on my good friend and neighbor Diann to pray.

August 29, 1986 Exodus 30:1-10 tells exactly how the altar was to be built and what was to be sacrificed on it. Nothing else except what the Lord described was to be offered on it. If I need to take care of something at the altar, it is to no avail to try to offer something else! He wants the area He wants! I know I've got to just pray through and get it settled once and for all.

Lord, I committed my life to You years ago and told You that I wanted You to keep it NO MATTER WHAT else I might say in a weak moment. I know I've been holding on to something that has come between You and me. I want it very much, as You know, and my heart is breaking to give it up. I think I can't ***stand*** *to give it up, but I* ***will****. Part of me wants guarantees—promises from You that I'll get something better in place of this void—ah! Revelation! I* ***WILL! YOU!!*** *You are truly the best gift! And Lord, even if I never experience the natural side of this as I long to, I will still give it up for You and receive You as my reward, my treasure, my everything.*

I'm having trouble making this thorough—but I'm asking You to search the recesses of my heart and soul and bring it ***all*** *to the light. I'm not sure I'm sorry—and that's such an important part. You don't just want the sacrifice—You want a contrite heart. I'm sorry for leaving* ***You****; at this point, that's all I can honestly say.*

You *are Life and my world should revolve around You. I want that—I need that. I want to know that You joy in me. Do you, Lord? I need to be loved completely—can You do that? Do you even want to? When I look at my situation, it makes me think You don't desire it since I can't experience it in the natural.*

Please show me, Lord.

You ***do*** *love me, even when I'm ugly and contrary. Please reveal Your mercy to me. It's new every morning. I want You. Love, Becky*

Gene used to call me Becca, which nobody had ever done before. Revelation 2:17 says that the Lord will give a new name written on stone to those who overcome. It made me feel so special to think that the Lord actually wanted to love me that intimately.

I struggled with wanting to make the Lord my delight, yet still having intense desires for a life with Gene. I knew that if I couldn't have Gene, only the Lord could change my desires. I read about people like Jacob and his mother Rebekah, who used deception to get what they wanted. God had already told them that Jacob would be over Esau, so they didn't even HAVE to devise their own schemes. I knew that what I wanted seemed like the very best possible for this earth—but I had determined that I would NOT take it with my own hands. I knew that rebelling would give me immediate gratification, but I would miss out on the long-term promise of God, which was worth waiting for. I kept asking the Lord to either give me Gene or change me. I thought that if He would allow me to be with Gene, I would be the happiest person on earth; if not, at least I wouldn't have to live with the guilt of taking it for myself.

I was coming to a new understanding of God's holiness. He wanted me to be holy like He is instead of trying to pull Him down to my level. He was showing me that all my goodness was like filthy rags. Experiencing His holy presence was a privilege I didn't want to give up—and sin couldn't go in. Having one foot in the world and one in the Lord was uncomfortable—like straddling a fence. I knew I would have problems in every area of my life if I continued to compromise.

At church during the month of September, the Lord sent people to share His love with me during a time when I felt totally unworthy of forgiveness, much less of the way He was wooing me back to His side. Although I tried to tell myself that they didn't know what they were talking about, He was still getting through to my fearful, hurting heart.

Early in the month, an older woman from our congregation walked up to me and told me that the Lord had shown her how much He loved me. I couldn't even begin to comprehend His great love and mercy towards me. He wanted me to know that He would never leave me or forsake me!

Another day later in the month when I was in the sanctuary playing the piano and working on the list of songs for worship service, the pastor's wife came through on her way to the church office. She started for the door behind me but stopped and came back and said, "The Lord is pleased with your heart and your music." I thought, "Oh, if only you knew what was in my heart, you wouldn't be saying that!" But her words echoed in my mind for days and weeks and even months later, giving me hope that perhaps the Lord was not through with me, after all, and that perhaps He would eventually be able to forgive me.

He did begin to speak to me again from His Word, too. At first, it was just to let me know that I had made the right decision by staying with Tracy and that He would honor that. I had been reading in Leviticus, which is not the first chapter in the Bible a person would think of in regard to marriage enrichment! Nevertheless, the Holy Spirit began to speak to me right where I was reading, where the Word tells what would happen when the Israelites entered the Promised Land. Leviticus 19:23-25 reads, "When you enter the land and plant any kind of fruit tree, regard its fruit as forbidden. For three years you are to consider it forbidden; it must not be eaten. In the fourth year all its fruit will be holy, an offering of praise to the Lord. But in the fifth year you may eat its fruit. In this way your harvest will be increased. I am the Lord your God."

When I first read this passage, I wasn't sure I was really supposed to apply it to my situation. I wasn't even sure I wanted to! Marriage certainly wasn't mentioned in these verses, yet something inside let me know the Lord was speaking to my heart. I really believed the Lord was trying to tell me something about fruit of another kind.

I could see that I would be wise to let things take their time and season where the growth of my marriage was concerned. I thought the Lord was telling me that even when I began to see "fruit" in Tracy—when I saw changes or small moves towards loving me—I was not to cling to it or make demands or begin to have expectations. I was to wait until the fullness of time for us when the Lord would perform the miracle of the seed: fruit from obedience to Him.

It is hard to describe how I could be so angry with God, telling Him I wouldn't believe or trust Him since He'd "led me astray" in the first place, while at the same time hearing His Words of promise and clinging to them. I think it was because deep down, I knew He had never really let me down before. I knew He was faithful and the Only One I could ever trust. He was my only hope. I was willing to accept the idea that I would never find true love in my relationship with Tracy and that obedience to the Lord was worth giving up any hope of happiness here on earth. If that was what it meant to serve the Lord faithfully, then that was what I was going to do. Still, there was no assurance of God's goodness. Tracy had prayed years earlier on the night he proposed that I would learn to fear the Lord, and amazingly, his prayer was answered in a way that would affect our entire family from then on. It was only the fear of the Lord that kept me from throwing all propriety to the wind and wrecking our lives.

Next, the Lord led me to the verse in Titus, where the older women are exhorted to teach the younger women to love their husbands and children. I already knew how to love my children and didn't feel it was something that needed to be taught! But I had never noticed before that loving was something that COULD be taught! I let the Lord know that if it were possible, it was something that only He could do. I didn't feel I had an older woman to go to so I could learn how to love Tracy. Rather, I told God that He would have to teach me what to do.

He was faithful to do exactly that, by impressing on my mind that He wanted me to begin to do for Tracy what I wanted to do for Gene. It made me physically ill to even consider that as an option! I didn't WANT to act loving towards Tracy! I hated hypocrisy and games, and to act lovingly towards him seemed like the ultimate deception and farce!

Yet I was sure that was what the Lord was saying, so I began to take very small steps towards doing things that I wanted desperately to do for the man I really loved. I started considering what Tracy might like to eat when planning my menus. I tried to wear clothes that I was sure he liked to see on me. I began to ask what he wanted to do when we had some free time. I was pleasant when talking to him and tried to really listen when he shared, too. It was difficult, and I was extremely uncomfortable going through the motions when there were no feelings to back up my actions, but I was obedient outwardly. Inwardly, I still wished to be free from my legal contract of marriage with Tracy. In God's eyes, only death or Tracy's unfaithfulness would free me from the covenant we had made before Him.

One thing that made it so difficult was that Gene and I kept calling and writing to each other. One night after Gene had called me, and I was more lonesome than ever, I actually pictured Tracy dead. I saw him in his coffin and visualized his parents crying at the funeral. That got my attention! I knew how wicked it was for me to wish him gone, and I realized that I had to get a grip on my thoughts. I cried out to God again, begging Him to make a way for me to be with Gene, sensing Him saying that He understood all I was feeling yet also knowing He could not and would not make exceptions to His Word. I somehow found a way to keep going, but I was miserable.

Just because I'd had an encouraging word from the Lord that seemed to be His promise to me, everything did not automatically become easy and smooth! I still struggled with intense feelings for Gene. At times it threatened to undo me totally. If it hadn't been for the effect of God's Word in my life, both the foundation I had up to that point and the continual seeking Him, I would never have made it out of the pit.

September 22, 1986 In Numbers 14, ten Israeli spies told the people how big the enemy was. Even though the land was flowing with milk and honey, the people were too afraid to fight. So the Lord didn't let any of those men enter the Promised Land. I mustn't look at the "land of promise" and be fainthearted, saying it's too hard. Instead of looking at the obstacles, I should be obedient each step of the way. I sure don't want to wander around and end up missing the promise. I know I can't fight the battle on my own! I also can't take it all on at once, but one enemy at a time!

I can't say I'd be better off back in bondage, without the promise. ***Believe*** *He wants good for me and that's it's worth the journey.*

September 25, 1986 Numbers 21 relates how Israel had to fight the inhabitants of the Promised Land before they could take it for their own. The enemies living there wouldn't let them pass through peaceably, and the Lord didn't want the Israelites to leave any survivors. It's a joke to think my enemy will let me just pass through peaceably on my journey. He hates me and wants to plunder and kill me! SO, I should be ready to do battle and take the land God has given me. There is no room for passivity—I know what the Lord has promised me, and I'm going to possess it. I won't leave any survivors to torment me or hassle me or steal my peace. You can't strike peace with the enemy. The only way to have peace is to do away with him all the way!

October 3, 1986 Blessings come through obedience. I might think I'm giving up a blessing, but actually I don't need what the enemy makes look good—I need the will of God!

I was moving from being a victim to being a fighter. But my desire to hold on to Gene was prolonging the battle and the agony. I was seeing that if I wanted any rest from the war, I would need to put the sword to the relationship, including the continued calls and letters. The pleasure they brought no longer outweighed the agony.

God was giving me clearly defined boundaries, showing me what He was giving me, as well as what He was NOT giving me. It helped with the confusion and brought security.

He was also showing me a huge lack in my life. I had always thought I honored God, but I was neglecting that by withholding honor from Tracy. That had to change.

I remember lying in bed one December night, really battling the feeling of having to give my all while receiving nothing in return. It was hard for me to think of having no hope of a *love* relationship—just being committed out of duty alone wasn't enough. Then, I heard the Spirit say, "With Jesus, all things are possible." I thought, "Yeah!" and began to pray for Tracy to be able to love me in the way I needed it. I rejoiced in hope!

But the enemy does not give up without a fight of his own. During this time, Gene was working on a recording project and invited me to come see him so I could sing backup on one of the songs. It was one he hadn't really liked as well as some of his other tunes, but during his stay with us, I had helped him rewrite a couple of lines and told him it was my favorite. He ended up making it the title song for his project, and he felt it was only right that I should participate. I made up my mind to go, even though I knew it was foolish. I tried to tell myself nothing would happen—that I had proven I was intent on doing what was right.

But even when Tracy expressed concern about my making the trip, I insisted on having my way. I used anything he had ever done wrong to try to gain leverage, and he didn't fight me on it. Things were still distant between us, and he felt I was already too busy, but since it was during my Christmas break from college, he didn't feel he had a legitimate reason to insist that I stay home. By this time in our marriage, I had already used manipulation and bullying enough to get my way on almost every issue, and my disrespect for Tracy over so many years had resulted in a lack of resolve on his part. He had no recourse but to watch me leave, and I am certain that he was more aware of my affection for this friend than either of us wanted to admit.

I left exhilarated! I listened to pop radio stations all the way, and every love song caused my heart to soar in anticipation of the reunion we would have. I was so distracted that I didn't notice a speed limit sign posted near some construction. I was pulled over and got the first speeding ticket of my entire life! Even that didn't bring me out of my daze, though; thankfully, I encountered no further problems on the way.

Gene had arranged for me to stay with his sister, but shortly after my arrival, he came to greet me. It was all I'd dreamed of and more. We talked late into the night, holding each other again while the feelings came back in full force.

We spent hours in the studio, recording the title song for his project and jamming with the equipment there. I was thrilled to be part of something that was such an integral part of him, and even more so since he'd included the song because of my belief in the power it held. Even during this time, both of us still looked to the Lord and wanted Him to use us with the gifts He'd given us. We wanted to reach other people, regardless of how confused we were ourselves. God's goodness didn't change just because we were playing with fire. Even His gifts were still in operation in our lives. There was an anointing on the music that I believed would touch others and set them free.

On New Year's Eve, I went with him to a local club where he was employed to play the piano. We laughed for hours as we recalled conversations of people around us, shallow people who had nothing better to discuss than their most recent plastic surgeries! It was as though we shared a special secret of what life was really about, and it had nothing to do with true life in the Lord; it had everything to do with the love we'd found in one another. It was bittersweet, cherishing each moment together, yet knowing it would come to a close again in just a few short days.

I got my second traffic ticket of my life that night. In a daze from the emotions I was feeling, I actually turned LEFT on a red light! Since I was coming out of a club, the officers who pulled me over were very thorough to ensure I had not been drinking, which I hadn't. It's almost funny now to look back—I wouldn't have even considered drinking alcohol, yet I was flirting with the idea of having an affair! And I don't believe it was a coincidence that I received two tickets during that trip, either. If I'd been where I was supposed to be, *with whom* I was supposed to be, the tickets never would have been issued. I was beginning to understand the umbrella of God's protection and my husband's covering just a little bit. Interestingly enough, I've never had another ticket since then!

For me, the most precious time with Gene was one night when he took me back to his sister's house. She was gone, and he didn't have a key to get in. We waited quite awhile outside then finally decided I would just go back to his place for the night. Amazingly, we still didn't have sex, but we slept in the same bed and talked for hours. He held me, and I felt more loved during those moments than I ever had in my entire life. He knew exactly what to say and when to listen. We talked about my marriage, about our music, about our hopes and dreams, and about our love. We told silly stories. We laughed and cried and lay in silence. Even though I knew I would have to let go, I still cherished every moment, knowing I would never forget the comfort I'd found in his arms.

Even through the tenderness, one day I saw a little glimpse of something that should have been a wake-up call for me, but I chose to ignore it. We had planned to get together early one morning to work on some music we wanted to co-write, but I felt guilty for not spending any time with his sister. I stayed longer that morning chatting with her than I had intended; I think I was trying to convince her I was really there with innocent intentions, even though she had to have been suspicious of my relationship with Gene.

When I finally arrived at Gene's place, he was extremely testy and moody. I knew he was upset that I was so late arriving, but I thought I'd appease him with a big breakfast. He wasn't appeased, and his temper, although kept at bay, was just under the surface. I explained why I was late and tried to make it up to him, but it was a cloud over our entire day. Even that night, he was still sullen about it. I didn't want to see anything negative about him, so I just took the blame, feeling I should have gone on over early or called to let him know why I was late.

The remaining days spent together were a conflict of emotions. I was tormented with how much he seemingly met my needs because I knew I couldn't really have him. Before the time was over, though, I was miserable and wondered what in the world I had been thinking of. Even though we weren't having sex, we were being entirely too intimate, and I was giving my entire heart to him again. One afternoon while he was in the shower, I screamed at the top of my lungs, asking myself what in the world I was doing there! I prayed and cried, asking the Lord to help me get out of the mess I'd made. My trip home was not full of anticipation as the trip down had been; rather, I was full of despair and heartache, dreading going back home. I was desperate for relief from the bondage I was in.

I felt guilty and dirty and unworthy of forgiveness. Once again I was at a time when I believed God would never be able to forgive me, because I really knew better than to put myself back in such a situation. Still, when I got back home, Tracy commented that I looked younger and refreshed—even glowing. I wanted to scream at him that it was because I'd been with someone who knew how to love me, but there was no fight left in me.

I began praying desperately for the Lord to send Gene a wife so that his needs would be met—partially because I wanted him to be happy and fulfilled and partially because I knew it would help him stop calling me, which only prolonged our misery.

> *January 4, 1987 I'm starting a new year; one that is requiring many changes of me. I must have a change of desire, will, hopes, thought patterns, etc.: in short, I must learn again to die to self. I can't ask myself what I* ***want****—I must instead yield. But what does that leave me? I must have vision, purpose, direction, and the will to live my life as it* ***is****.*
>
> *I have talents and abilities and ample responsibility—but where is the* ***meaning****? I know I must seek to serve instead of being served.*
>
> *Real meaning comes from the Lord—if I'm not finding my joy in Him, then how can I convince anyone else to try Him?!*
>
> *Can I find a quiet time to* ***really reach*** *Him?*
>
> *The bottom line is that ONLY He can really satisfy me and meet my needs. Nobody else can do it fully—they'll always hurt me and fall short. It's time for me to get close to Him again and find contentment.* ***He alone meets my needs****.*

Tracy wanted very much to please me, and he asked what
he could do to make me satisfied. I knew there wasn't anything he could just *do*. The Lord gave me a word of wisdom, which I shared with Tracy: that he should be the man God called him to be and I should be the woman God called me to be and we would both be happy! So simple, yet so profound! As we began to refocus that way, it started setting us both free to live unto the Lord and strive to please *Him*, not each other.

During this time, I still felt like I was just going through the motions with Tracy. I didn't want to be that way; I really wanted to change from the inside. I was so discouraged, though. I knew pursuing a relationship with Gene wasn't what I needed to do, but being lonely was agony. I kept looking to the Lord, but He seemed so distant.

I even felt like a prostitute in my own bed with my husband. That was because I had given my heart to someone else, and I was wrong. It was my own fault that I felt unfaithful when I was with my husband, and it was one more area where I needed to repent and be cleansed.

*January 7, 1987 I Kings 8:39b "Then hear from heaven, your dwelling place. Forgive and act; deal with each man according to all he does . . . for you alone know the hearts of all men." Ah, Lord—You are **so** big. Please search my heart and get rid of the garbage—make me really clean **inside**; then the outside will be clean. My heart truly wants You most of all—only You can satisfy.*

*January 8, 1987 Solomon's kingdom reminds me of the Lord's—how pleasant just to be near Him—it causes us to want to **give** to Him, also.*

*Can I make my home a place that my family loves to be? That it would seem a privilege to be a part of our family? I **want** to!*

*January 10, 1987 The Lord **WILL** do what He's promised, and it will be the **greatest** blessing I could ever have. I just need to trust and obey. When I start to doubt, sin isn't far behind. Lord, help me to trust You and let You bring it to pass.*

January 12, 1987 I Kings 17:7-16 tells about the widow who had only enough flour and oil to make one more meal for herself and her son. Elijah asked her to make him a loaf first, so she did. Miraculously, there was more flour and oil every day until the famine was over! If she'd taken the first loaf for herself or her son, then there would have been no more flour and oil. Blessings and provisions come when we OBEY!

Really, when you're going to die anyway, you might as well risk one meal for the chance of life! When we really look at a situation, as the Lord asks us to give up something, it is VERY small compared to what we're going to get back!

The Lord was wooing me gently, letting me know that He was going to take care of me and I should not leave any options open. He was showing me that He wanted *every* area. I didn't want to have the Lord make a judgment about me that I did well in following Him—except for this one area. I wanted Him to be pleased with all of my life; in fact, that was coming to mean more to me than anything I could cling to! And I knew that whatever I wrongly held on to would also make my children stumble, so I was surrendering to a greater degree.

We hear people in twelve-step programs talk about taking things one day at a time, and I could relate to that. I didn't need to try to have enough love, hope, joy, etc. for the rest of my life—just for one day! That was good news!

> *February 19, 1987 Lord, You have been speaking to me for about 13 years—always faithful to show me Your ways of truth. At times my heart has been good soil; other times not very fertile; sometimes even hard.*
>
> *Right now I desire to be pliable—and not just pliable, but also rich, ready ground that will receive the Word and go on to produce a crop.*
>
> *Lord, please watch over this Word today and don't let anything or anyone snatch it away before it's rooted in me. Let the roots go deep and bring forth fruit.*
>
> *I'll do my part—yielding to You completely so the seed can get in. You're a* ***good*** *gardener! Much more experienced than I! I trust You to plant, tend, and cultivate my soul to make the best of my life.*

> *March 5, 1987 I Chronicles 18:4 "David captured a thousand of [the king of Zobah's] chariots, seven thousand charioteers and twenty thousand foot soldiers. He hamstrung all but a hundred of the chariot horses." When we fight our enemies, we want to be sure they can't rise up against us again—we want to subdue them while they're in our power.*
>
> *David hamstrung all but 100 of the chariot horses of his enemy. Chariots were a symbol of power and mobility. A chariot is nothing without the horse to pull it, though! By making the horses disabled and powerless, he was keeping the enemy under control.*
>
> *What gives the strength to my enemy? What feeds it? What carries it along? My thoughts and words. So I must hamstring them—make them powerless—cut off the source of power that causes me to sin.*

Again, God was showing me that it was crucial to stop the correspondence with Gene. Every call and letter added fuel to the fire. But it was still a battle I was fighting with myself. I remembered that King David had been punished for taking a census of his fighting men, and it was only because he thought that would tell him whether or not he would win against his enemies. I thought of Gideon, who had conquered his enemy with only 300 men!

The Lord didn't want me to consider my own resources to determine whether I'd win or not—or whether to fight and attack the enemy or not. I just needed to obey His voice. The arm of flesh would *fail* me, but His arm was stretched out to me.

When I wondered whether good or evil would win, I realized it depended on which one was fed! I needed to run to the Lord, because He was a strong tower. I needed to refrain from making demands on Tracy that he couldn't keep. I needed to walk by faith, not by what I could see with my eyes.

I was familiar with the story of the Lord telling King Solomon that he could ask whatever he wanted of God and it would be given to him. He asked for wisdom to rule the people, not blessings for himself. The New Testament also teaches that we may ask God for anything and He'll give it to us. I knew that what I asked for tested my character. What I was starting to want most was to be closer to Him—to know Him better—to have Him for my best friend.

Two Scriptures were of great comfort to me. II Chronicles 16:9 reads, "For the eyes of the Lord range throughout the earth to strengthen those whose hearts are fully committed to him." Then II Chronicles 15:17 says, "Although he did not remove the high places from Israel, Asa's heart was fully committed to the Lord all his life." I knew that even though I still struggled, my heart was reaching for Jesus. I wanted my heart to be an open door to Him, even if He had to "meddle" with it sometimes to make me clean.

Gradually, there were small changes at home. As weeks passed, I noticed that being in the same room with Tracy didn't nauseate me. I realize that might sound far-fetched, but before that time, it was actually how I felt. I despised him so much that I couldn't stand to even be in the same room with him! Eventually, I discovered that I was even starting to enjoy some of the things he had to say. I was starting to have a small amount of affection for him—not that it was passionate or anywhere near being the kind of "in love" feelings I'd had for Gene, but still, we were experiencing a sense of camaraderie that had been missing for years.

In time, I even began to feel love for Tracy; again, it wasn't the kind of earth-shaking, heart-throbbing, body-tingling chemistry I longed for, but there was a sense of friendship developing that was pleasant and made the tasks of serving him not quite so dreary. We had a long way to go, but for the first time in many years, I felt a slight stirring of joy as what I'd been hoping for was actually being experienced to a small degree.

Something very interesting began to happen to Tracy during this time. He had actually given up ever trying to please me years earlier since I had repeatedly rejected his efforts. Now, he could sense that I had absolutely no expectations of him whatsoever. It didn't matter what he did, and in fact, it didn't even matter whether or not he did anything at all! This began to set him free and allowed him to actually begin showing me love in small ways at first, then slowly in deeper ways. The truth was, he had never quit loving me even during all those years when I was hard and proud and unbending. It just hadn't been worth the effort to show me how he felt when the attempts were rejected. Now he could display his feelings without having them thrown back in his face, so it was becoming easier for him to express himself. The time hadn't come yet for our love to really blossom, but at least seeds were being planted that had some chance of making it to harvest!

I continued to serve the Lord at church, leading worship, teaching children's church, helping teach adult Sunday school at times, and helping with youth group. My dear friend, Anne Matlock, was helping me run the day care so I could keep home-schooling the children and attending classes at the college. Tracy stayed busy helping with our own children in the evenings by giving them their baths and tucking them into bed. He also scrubbed bathrooms and floors and did the vacuuming. I still did the cooking and dishes and laundry. We were busy, which was probably good during the time when I was struggling to get over my love for Gene.

He and I tried not to contact each other, but it was difficult. I would do well for a few days or weeks, but he would break down and either call or write. Then it would flip, and just when he was starting to get victory, I would begin to miss him to the point I didn't think I could stand it, and I would be the one to contact him. It was a vicious cycle, trying to do what was right, yet finding it almost impossible to completely sever the ties.

During this time, one Scripture in Hebrews caused a war to wage in my mind. It is found in the sixth chapter, beginning with verse 4. It says, "It is impossible for those who have once been enlightened, who have tasted the heavenly gift, who have shared in the Holy Spirit, who have tasted the goodness of the word of God and the powers of the coming age, if they fall away, to be brought back to repentance, because to their loss they are crucifying the Son of God all over again and subjecting him to public disgrace." I didn't realize that there is a big difference between "falling away" and "falling down." Everyone falls down in some way; the Bible tells us that anyone who claims he doesn't sin is calling God a liar! But falling away from the faith is an entirely different issue. I was so guilt-ridden, I couldn't see the difference. I was more certain than ever that I would meet with some sudden and horrendous death. I knew I had to get Gene out of my system, but again, we found it almost impossible not reach out to one another.

When his recording project was finished, I played "our" song over and over, reminiscing about our time together, yet torturing myself further with the unattainable. I began praying even more fervently that the Lord would send him a wife so he wouldn't need me anymore. I thought that if he could quit calling, I might be able to leave him alone, too.

He left on a Christian singing tour and met a young lady who would later become his wife. I was slowly letting go of him, yet there was still a fantasy in my mind and emotions that somehow we would be together. I would turn quickly in a crowd, thinking I'd seen him go by. I'd see a car that looked like his, and my heart would skip a beat. I'd get a letter in the mail with writing similar to his, and my breath would catch. And when he called me, all the feelings would return, but they were usually less intense than at first. I was relieved when he did finally marry and happy for him when I learned that they were expecting their first child.

I continued to work on my degree and serve the Lord at church, gradually accepting His forgiveness and love. He gently showed me areas of intolerance for others, and He faithfully chipped away at my self-righteousness. He reminded me of many Scriptures on grace and mercy. One that blessed me during that time was when Peter asked the Lord if he should forgive people seven times. The Lord replied that we should forgive seventy times seven! It dawned on me that if He expected that kind of forgiveness from us, then He would certainly do at least that much or more.

I also began to see that if I had actually turned my back on the Lord to the point described in Hebrews 6, then it wouldn't even bother me that I had done so! It is not an easy thing to lose your salvation! I slowly felt restored and definitely looked upon others with more compassion for their weaknesses and sins. I was grateful for the Lord's tolerance, even more so than when I'd first believed. I was starting to comprehend that since He had saved me when I was a sinner, then after making me His very own child, He would do even more to accept and love and change me.

Months passed, then years. I spoke to Gene on occasion, and I was slowly feeling I could be a friend to him again. I knew I never wanted to go back to a place of agony like I'd known before, and I was starting to see how very ignorant I'd been. I read a book titled *Women Who Love Too Much*, by Robin Norwood, and it was a real eye-opener. I saw for the first time that having grown up with an alcoholic father had changed what was "normal" for me. Chaos and dependency were what I knew, and Tracy seemed boring compared to all that emotional upheaval! Gene needed me desperately, and even more than his ability to share on an intimate level conversationally, the intensity of his personality and the attention he required were what I had been accustomed to as a child. I felt needed and wanted, and he knew how to speak the language that made me feel loved. I was beginning to see how the cycle of dependency and codependency I'd grown up with had affected my relationships as an adult. When I realized the parallels between Gene and my father, I was shocked; Gene even had a drinking problem! His demanding neediness kept things stirred up, and I could relate to it. I knew how to deal with it, whereas I hadn't known how to deal with someone like Tracy who served instead of demanding.

I didn't want to admit it, but I was starting to comprehend that Tracy was actually exactly what I needed! He was stable, consistent, and solid as a rock! He worked hard to provide for the children and me. He was not jealous or demanding, and he gave me lots of freedom. I started to see that one of the reasons it seemed as if Gene met my needs was that he didn't have a job and was available to romance me. If Tracy had been home all the time, without a job, he might have had more time to meet my needs, too! If I'd had to depend on Gene to take care of the children and me, what would we have eaten? Those were hard things to face, but I've always loved the truth, and I couldn't ignore the way these facts were starting to stack up.

I was also facing the fact that since chaos felt normal to me, that's one of the reasons I constantly pushed Tracy into fighting with me. His nature was to keep peace, not to bicker, and even though I was miserable fighting all the time, it was what I knew. The conflict was what I felt comfortable with, even though it wasn't healthy.

With that realization came a greater appreciation for Tracy. We were starting to develop a friendship that we had briefly known when we first met. I had to respect him for his hard work, and I was grudgingly willing to see that it was his way of showing me his love. I still would have preferred tender words and attention, but at least it was a start.

As I continued to release him from any obligation to meet my needs, mostly because I still didn't think he *could*, Tracy became more and more free to show his love for me. I was amazed that he had never quit caring for me, even though I was horrid to him. He had such perseverance! Again, I had to admire him for that. We were moving towards a new phase in our marriage, and though it wasn't the passion I longed for, we were at least friendlier to each other. Our children needed us to be stable, and I had always wanted a good life for them, so I resigned myself even more to just surviving and doing what had to be done.

Gene and I still wrote now and then, and I had just finished a letter to him one day. Instead of mailing it, I had gotten busy and accidentally left it out on the end table in the living room. I had served dinner and was just drying my hands from finishing the dishes, when I saw Tracy with the letter in his hands. Everything froze! Our three children were playing in the next room, but I couldn't hear them. The light was glaring off of Tracy's glasses, so I couldn't see his eyes to get a feel for what he was thinking. I remember lifting my hand to my head and noticing the smell of Joy dishwashing soap. I wracked my brain to remember what I'd written, knowing I no longer expressed my love to Gene, yet having the sickening realization that in the letter Tracy held, I had referred to the way my relationship with Gene had been during his stay with us and the months that followed. The metallic taste of fear and guilt filled my mouth, and I didn't know what to do or say. I had never before, nor have I since, heard such silence. Time stood still as I waited for Tracy to speak.

Of course, he wanted to know what I was referring to in my letter. I knew I was faced with a decision: the letter wasn't too explicit, so I probably could have talked my way out of it. I was terrified of being rejected and abandoned, even though I wasn't close to Tracy emotionally. The fear was paralyzing, yet I also realized in those split seconds that it would be better to be rejected for the truth than to live a lie any longer. Since I hated playing games and hungered for the truth, I decided that my only recourse was to tell Tracy what had happened. Then if he still wanted to be with me, it would be based on who and what I really was, not who he thought I was. So I found myself telling Tracy exactly what my relationship with Gene had been.

I don't always suggest that wives and husbands tell each other everything. That is a decision that must be made in each individual case, usually with much prayer and some sound counsel. But for Tracy and me, it was the best thing we could have done. Once I had shared with him, he also had some things he wanted to share with me. We laid everything on the table, and we discovered that great burdens were lifted for both of us. Tracy still wanted to be with me, and we knew it would be a long road to build the trust between us again, but we decided to start to build, with Jesus and honesty as our foundation.

Scripture teaches us that if we look upon another with lust in our hearts, we have already committed adultery in our hearts. That is totally true. Yet I think the enemy uses that Scripture to make some people think they might as well go ahead and do it since they have already committed adultery in their hearts. That simply is not true! If I had actually become one flesh with Gene through sex, it would have been even more difficult to get through what was coming our way. The fact that I had not gone that far made a difference. There can still be forgiveness if two people have become one in the flesh, but it does complicate the issues. You truly DO become one with that person. It was hard enough that we were one in our souls—to have become one flesh, too, would have created a bond that would have been even more difficult to overcome. It also would have made it more difficult for Tracy, my wounded spouse.

And he *was* wounded, even though he wanted to stay with me. As days went by, I saw a side of Tracy I'd never seen before. He was devastated. Having a vague sense that something was wrong when it was taking place all those months earlier was not the same as now being confronted with the awful truth. One evening, he was so overcome with grief that he got in his pickup and drove off without a word. He peeled out, squealing his tires, and I was afraid he would kill himself. My guilt was back in full force, because whenever I looked at him, I saw the pain in his blue eyes and knew I had put it there. It wasn't just guilty *feelings*, but *true* guilt from wronging him and not keeping my covenant with him. Even though I had told myself I wanted to be free from him, I still feared what would happen if he actually took his own life, and I didn't want to be responsible for that. Relief flooded over me when I heard his truck pull back into the driveway hours later!

He forgave me, but it took time for him to be able to get the victory over his thoughts. He wanted to hurt Gene, yet he was also strangely forgiving of him, too. Tracy knew deep down that as a husband he didn't meet my needs, and he felt partially responsible for my being vulnerable when the temptation had hit me. Not very many men would have the kind of maturity to look at it like that, and he did endear himself to me for that attitude. This was one more thing that helped me believe that we might make it and possibly not be miserable the entire time. I was starting to see a tiny bit of fruit on the tree of our marriage, yet I heeded what the Lord had shown me about waiting to partake of it. I didn't want to scare Tracy away from continuing to make efforts to show me his love.

The Lord was doing a deep work in me, and although it was painful and not what I would have chosen, He was letting me see a part of His nature I'd never known before. As Tracy continued to love me unconditionally, I was coming to know the Lord's same love for me. It was an accurate view of how God looked at me—forgiven, loved, cherished, wanted, no matter what I'd done. It met a need in me I didn't even know I had! It was something deeper and more crucial than any romantic notion I'd ever longed for. Without my realizing it, God was bringing healing and comfort and peace to a deep place in my soul. I found old fears being replaced with assurance. I found my drive for perfection lessening, and a load was lifted from me since I didn't need to win or keep anyone. I could fall flat on my face, and someone would still be there to pick me up, clean me off, and help me keep going. It was precious and worth all the energy and introspection that rebuilding our trust was taking.

5. Throwing a Royal Fit

You've already seen evidence of the way I could really "let go" and pitch a fit in order to try to get my way! Soap opera stars had nothing on me when it came to manipulation! By this time in our life together, I was no longer trying to use tears or anger to manipulate Tracy because I didn't think there was any hope of getting my way! But before our marriage could become a real relationship where both Tracy and I were giving and receiving, there was still a major character flaw in me that had to be dealt with. The desire to control everything had to go! That tendency is quite common in adult children of alcoholics; their childhoods are typically so chaotic that they strive for a controlled environment where they can protect themselves.

Understanding *why* I struggled with control issues, though, was not an excuse to continue the behavior. The first step towards change was realizing I needed it, and the Lord was up for the job of showing me! He wanted me to learn that I could trust Him to take care of me—that I didn't have to stand up for my own rights or throw fits or go overboard to control situations. He used my situation with Gene to help me start to face my own shortcomings and begin to see how I could learn to be content even when my circumstances were not ideal.

> *September 28, 1989 My desire must be for the Lord, not for a husband who will be all the things I need. [The Lord] has been merciful to me by NOT giving me what I thought (in my foolishness) I wanted. He is truly gracious and slow to anger.*
>
> *Philippians 4:12 says, "I know what it is to be in need, and I know what it is to have plenty. I have learned the secret of being content in any and every situation." Then comes the familiar verse 14, "I can do everything through him who gives me strength." Lord, teach me the secret of being content. Surely it has to do with looking to You instead of to people or things to make me happy. Show me that You are really enough!*

Being content meant I had to learn to let go of Gene, my dreams, and my own plans for my life. The work the Lord was doing in my marriage was only a fraction of what He wanted to do in Tracy and me as individuals. He wanted us to live a life of abandonment to Him, and I had much to learn about what that really was. It was going to entail learning to give up my rights in many areas and releasing people from my control.

It used to really bother Tracy that I would often complain in stores and restaurants. I felt I was paying for goods and services, and I should be satisfied no matter what. If that didn't happen, I let everybody know about it and made enough noise until somebody would finally give me a satisfying outcome. The Lord began to soften me and help me see the needs of the people on the other end of my complaints. I learned to either voice my complaints in a nicer way or just let them go. I began to see that people are more important than being right. I needed to consider others rather than continuing to live a life that centered on my own needs!

Next I began to let go of unsatisfactory outcomes in business dealings that I couldn't change. My time as a busy mother and teacher didn't allow me to write the letters, contact the proper authorities, and get satisfaction for every situation that went wrong. But it was painful for me to let go of these things! For example, a few years ago, we had siding installed on our three-story house. Supposedly, this company was offering a special: in order to train their workers, they would sell us the siding at wholesale, and we would have no labor expenses. Even at wholesale cost, it was still a huge expenditure for our budget, and we really ran the numbers carefully before buying. The salesman watched as we worked and budgeted and considered the purchase, and he told us that even though he couldn't just make blanket statements for all houses, he *could* say that putting siding on *our* house would save us 40% in our heating expenses. He knew we were making our decision based on that information.

Well, when our heating bills began to come in the next winter, we discovered that we had saved only 2% in usage! I tracked it over many months, but the average did not go up, even though temperatures were similar to the year before.

I tried contacting the company, and I also complained to the Kansas Attorney General. I discovered that this Texas-based company was delinquent in their taxes required to work in Kansas. I even spoke with an attorney, but since the company was in Texas, any litigation would have to take place there, so he wasn't willing to take the case. Since we didn't have a written promise of savings, we couldn't do much. But I simply couldn't let go of it! I would get angry all over again every time I thought about it. I picked up more information at the Kansas State Fair on how to file a complaint about a company. I phoned a television station in Wichita to see about having them investigate the company! Even today when I think about it, I can almost feel my blood pressure rising! Ridiculous to you, perhaps, but it's just one more example of how hard it is for me to let go when I believe I've been taken advantage of!

I made a vow long ago NOT to allow people, especially men, to mistreat me, and it takes all the grace of God I can access simply to let go of things like this. I used to have files full of information on realtors who wronged us, letters to editors, etc.—all things that still irk me if I allow myself to dwell on them!

So I don't! I have to practice letting go over and over! I ask the Lord to continue to change me, and I relinquish my rights again. I confess out loud that I trust my husband to look out for the best interests of our family. I remind myself that in eternity, it won't matter! I remember that it isn't worth the emotional energy required to nurse the grudge! I LET GO!

Then I had to learn to laugh at myself when I couldn't let go of stuff or projects! Case in point: one summer recently, one of my goals was to deep clean the craft/game/sewing/junk room. While two of our children, Benjamin and Ashley, were gone on their mission trips, the youngest two children, Justin and Anna, helped me tackle the job. We sorted every little game piece from about twenty-five or thirty games. We sorted all the cards we owned—there were ten full decks plus a whole crate of extras left over. We organized all the craft supplies into neat cubbies and plastic tubs and baskets. The real kicker, though, was the puzzles. We own (or owned, past tense!) over forty puzzles. Some were for younger children, with only sixty-some odd pieces. Others had over 500 pieces.

Was it good enough to me to just throw out loose pieces? Could I toss them all and start over with new puzzles? Emphatically, NO! I had to put together almost ALL of those puzzles so we'd know which ones were complete, which ones were missing pieces, which ones were worth saving, which ones were missing too many to save, ETC. I didn't feel as if I could throw out puzzles I didn't like until we put them together to make sure no extra pieces would be tossed that went to another puzzle I did like! It took us over two weeks!

Tracy really thought I had lost my mind. He grumbled about not knowing why I didn't just toss them all and start over. He didn't tell me I HAD to, though, so I kept working. I did end up tossing quite a few of the puzzles after we were sure they didn't contain any "good" pieces. I love puzzles, and Justin and I really enjoyed the time spent putting them together. Yes, it disrupted the living room, dining room, and kitchen for a while, but it was SO worth it to me! I know I could have spent the time doing other things—like writing this rough draft or expanding my business—but I received such a sense of satisfaction, knowing things were orderly again.

And speaking of having things orderly, one thing I like to do is roll the towels. You know, roll them and put them in cute baskets or open cabinets in the bathroom. I know, it's not in the same league with rolling out the red carpet for royalty—my "prince"—but it makes a difference at my house! It's my effort to be organized. Not *Better Homes and Gardens* quality, perhaps, but just a touch of elegance that helps me feel we're at least somewhat set apart from the animals!

I have stacks, too. Clean laundry, not put away. Clean clothes that had been put away, but I thought I was going to wear then changed my mind—stacked on top of the baskets of rolled towels because there wasn't time to go through all of it and put it away carefully. But the towels go there, so . . . another stack of towels. Another stack of clothes worn briefly. No female under twenty years old would remotely consider wearing it again, but at my age, having eight children, and with the—yes, **stacks** of dirty laundry, if the underarms don't stink, my clothes get worn again! There's a stack of clothes that might fit. I need to try them on. Another stack of clothes for the next garage sale. Another stack of clothes that are out of season, so they need to be stored.

Then there are the paper stacks. I save pictures the children have drawn for me, their special papers from school, love notes Tracy has written, awards of every kind, letters from friends—all memories that need to be tucked away. Then there are the stacks of payment stubs, payment plans, tax information, receipts, business correspondence, and personal correspondence. Also stacks of mail to go through, stacks of mail with to-do jobs, stacks of coupons.

I've always been a packrat; it is extremely hard for me to throw anything away that I MIGHT someday need for something. So I've got bits of craft materials, various sizes and shapes of cardboard boxes, and cardboard inserts from panty hose packages. Maybe it is born of fear, since as a child I saw that our family often did without. Maybe it's a creative twist to my personality, seeing something that can be made out of nothing. Maybe it's a desire to fill a hole in my soul with stuff. I don't know, but I do know we're in bondage to the stuff we have. It has to be maintained, and it takes up space and time and energy. So there are stacks that get moved to the craft/game/sewing/junk room, stacks that will have to wait, stacks that I probably don't really need since they can stay in the that room for months (okay, years!) without being touched!

It's an attempt to be organized. When I work at a job outside the home, they grow. Having so many children, they grow. Being too particular about how they're put away causes them to grow. Of course, there are the other jobs waiting to be done, such as baseboards being scrubbed, chair and stool legs having milk stains wiped off of them, mini blinds that practically need to be blasted clean with a high powered water hose (the fire department comes to mind!), etc. The jobs wait because I want them done a CERTAIN way, not slopped through! And we need to find time to tackle the projects properly!

But at least I'm rolling towels. And since that one little task helps me act more like a princess than a witch, Tracy is definitely feeling more like royalty!

Besides being fanatical about how jobs are done, I also tenaciously hold on to my plans. My dear friend of almost thirty years, Liz D'Urso, came to visit. She has several other friends in the area, so when she's at my house, it's always a stay-up-late kind of time, getting caught up on our families and ministries and life while we have the chance, because she's in high demand.

One evening while Liz was visiting, another friend stopped in on her way to Wichita. Rachelle Leonard brought her boyfriend and daughter Amelia by to chat, and they ended up staying a couple of hours for a lovely visit. She had been a little girl when Liz lived in our area, so it was fun to think back to times we'd shared years ago.

Well, I had planned to make cinnamon rolls for breakfast the next morning, and I suddenly realized that I hadn't started the dough yet. This was after 10:00 P.M. I decided to get it going in the bread maker and keep visiting. That would have been great, except that when I went in to roll out the dough over an hour later, I discovered that the metal pan hadn't been pushed down correctly, and there was no dough! Only dried out ingredients! SOOOOO, silly me, I had to go ahead and mix and knead the dough, let it rise, and bake those rolls! I didn't get much sleep, but I just couldn't bring myself to throw out the dough and forget it, even though Liz encouraged me to do so!

We can laugh about something so trivial, but the roots go deep. Something in me fears that if I let go of control or throw out something, I won't have what I need later. I feel I have to make life work according to plan! But I'm l earning that isn't my job!

When our oldest daughter Sara was a baby, I was a master of control! I got up at 6:00 A.M. to begin her scheduled activities for the day. At regulated times she ate, bathed, played in the playpen, slept, exercised, played on my lap, etc.! Nothing was left to chance! I thought that if I could just control the environment she grew up in, everything would be good for her. She would love and worship and serve Jesus, and her life would be good! And if other people would just let me at them, I could accomplish the same for them! Ugh! Thankfully, the outcomes of our lives are NOT dependent upon my ability to hold things together, after all!

Some people say that being late is also a form of control. I don't know; it's something I've struggled with my entire life! Even my periods were late! And all my birth babies were late! I would make my family late for church because I wanted to finish washing every last dish in the sink before we left—back to the idea of having to keep everything in order!

Tardiness really became a problem for me! The superintendent of our Christian school left notes in the boxes of teachers, because I was not the only one with this issue. Someone had pointed out to him that our employees had too many tardies, so he wanted feedback from us. He didn't know what he was asking for—I wrote him back PAGES of my struggles, reflections, and ideas about why I'm always late!

I've asked for prayer for this situation! But it really came home to me one summer when Anna was taking swimming lessons. Up to that time, she had LOVED everything about the water and had been splashing and swimming in it since she was a tiny baby. One day during lessons, there was some lightning, so they couldn't get in the water. Instead, they kept their little students under the covering of the building while they discussed water safety. For some reason, after that lesson, Anna started fearing the deep water! She refused to jump into the deep end or go off the diving board anymore. The teacher and I were working with her, trying to get her courage back up, but she was really scared.

I started encouraging her by telling her that the Spencers are BRAVE! We would "chant" this before lessons, driving to lessons, and before going to sleep at night! I wanted to bolster her confidence and get her back to her normal level of enjoyment at the pool. A couple of days before the last class, we were going to lessons again, and I said, "Anna, the Spencers are. . . . ?" I waited for her to fill in the blank. Instead of replying with "Brave," she shouted, "Late!"

How embarrassing that at five years of age, she already identified our family with that trait! But my control issues had affected every area of our family life!

Letting go is one of the hardest things we do as people, as mothers, and as wives. Steve and Annie Chapman recorded a song years ago that says, "The day your children learn to walk, they start to walk away from you . . . Can the sparrow ever learn to fly if the nest is all it knows? Can the arrow ever reach its mark by remaining in the bow? No, you have to let it go." How true! Yet it is so difficult to let go, and we find ourselves having to do it over and over and over again—even with the same situation or person!

Those of you who are mothers will identify with me when I describe the first nights of letting my babies sleep in their cribs instead of in the bassinet beside me. In the middle of the night, I would creep quietly into their room to place my finger close to their noses so I could feel the air being breathed in and out. Or I'd place my hand on their little chests or tummies for the same reason. It was so hard to let go of them to that degree—letting them stay in their own rooms out from under my watchful gaze! It was a time of learning that the Lord loves them even more than I do, and I can trust Him! He really doesn't need my help to watch them, even during sleep!

Well, letting go is part of life. We have to let go when our children take their first steps, when they start school (if we aren't home-schooling them), when they learn to drive, when they begin to date or court, and when they are married. And that list is only a start on the types of normal situations where we need to let go.

It is even harder to let go when our children have serious issues. Tracy and I have eight children, four of them birth children and four of them adopted. The adopted children are all siblings, and they had their own difficult experiences in early childhood. Their birth father was an alcoholic, and he was convicted of murdering their mother. So they came with great needs and issues. Our birth children were deeply affected by our decision to adopt, too, and there have been lots of emotions to work through. I especially have concerns for our two children who have struggled with addictions. But the truth is, I can't change the circumstances or the past, and I can't control the kids (especially those who are grown), so it's better to just release them to the Lord, Who loves them more than I do and Who CAN do something about their situations!

Sometimes giving up our rights and learning to be content means we will need to grieve and move on. I used to think that grief was just allowing myself to openly express my pain over a loss, but it can be defined as letting go of things that we were once attached to. It's a process that allows us to consciously and deliberately release people, goals, wishes, or ideas that we can no longer hold. Sometimes that's because they have been taken from us; other times it's because we've made our own decision to no longer allow them in our lives.

As we read the story of David and Bathsheba, we see an example of a woman who had to let go of much. Her story is told in 2 Samuel 11 and 12. She suffered great loss. First, she'd been alone while her husband, Uriah, was at war. We don't know how she felt about King David's advances towards her, but she was probably missing intimacy. Her husband was absent, and it was during her fertile time of month when the hormones being released cause a woman to be more "in the mood" than at other times of the month. She was probably lonesome for someone's arms around her and companionship, too. King David sent for her to come to him, and he lay with her. Perhaps she felt she had no choice; he was the king, after all. But she lost her self-respect and dignity. She lost her trustworthiness and faithfulness to her husband. She lost part of herself to David, as well.

Then, when David had Uriah killed, Bathsheba lost her husband. She lost every chance to make things right with him. She lost her home and all that was familiar to her as she moved into the palace. She probably lost her circle of friends for all practical purposes.

Finally, she lost the son she had conceived with David—God's judgment for David's sin. God later allowed her to be the mother of Solomon, the wisest man on earth—also the wealthiest, but no one could ever replace the son she lost.

Two summers ago, I had to give up something that was out of my control. I had a disagreement with a friend. She and I had been best of friends for many years—the kind of friends who had no secrets, who could understand each other's weaknesses, who had a history together for over twenty-five years, even across many miles!

Even though I had usually just overlooked flaws in her, and she had done the same for me, there was something going on over the summer that I knew needed to be addressed. She seemed to be at odds with everyone around her: her husband, the leadership of the church they had been attending, and many of her friends. In each situation, she felt the other people were always in the wrong. She seemed to need lots of grace to cover her own shortcomings, but she wasn't willing to give grace to others. This tendency was starting to affect our relationship, because I didn't want to continue to listen to her bad-mouthing others. I gently shared with her that all of us have areas needing improvement—we're all works in progress! I tried to help her see that we all fall short, but our love for one another covers a multitude of sins.

For some reason, she couldn't get past it. We ended up finding that our friendship couldn't withstand the pressures of my confronting her. Instead, my honesty with her on the issue was the beginning of the unraveling of our friendship.

My heart was wounded as I tried to let go, but I also had to battle anger. We had previously had some business dealings, and she still owed me several hundred dollars; when she gave me a final check, it was short about two hundred dollars. I had to absolutely FIGHT my flesh to just let it go! Over and over, I made the decision not to pick it back up again, to continue to love her and forgive her. It was totally against my nature to be bested, but the Lord was helping me put her above my feelings and pocketbook.

Through the months that followed, I continued to reach out to her. I sent notes in the mail with little gifts I thought she would enjoy. I called to wish her a happy birthday. I prayed continuously for her to be set free and that our relationship would be restored. All the time, I was asking God for grace to let her go.

Some other circumstances took place that finally caused her to let me know she had no desire to be my friend. She pointed out what she considered my error, but without the grace I was giving her for hers. Even then, I still wanted to be restored, but the day came when I realized she wasn't ready, and there was nothing I could do to change that. If she decides someday to be my friend again, the door is still open on my side. I don't take her rejection as a personal affront, because I know she is simply unhappy and at odds with many people. It isn't me; it's her own misery. I can't change that; I just had to grieve the loss and go on.

When I asked Gene to leave, it was a deliberate releasing of a person I knew I couldn't have if I wanted to please the Lord. But it took seven years for me to completely let go of the emotional attachment.

I don't know what causes some of us to hold on to things that aren't a blessing, that waste time or bring us down. Is it an intense desire to succeed? Is it fear of loss? Is it grieving over losses from the past? Probably some of all of the above! We hold on to things because we want to control the people or outcomes. We want to have our rights honored! We don't want to be wronged! But having a successful marriage—or even a successful life—will mean having to let go of some things.

The very fact that we can recognize we have issues is a good sign. Usually the first step to recovery or healing is realizing there is a problem. As long as we're willing to cooperate with God, He will continue to make everything beautiful in its time. And He is well able to do so! The quip is true: there is a God, and I'm not Him! While it is important to count our losses and allow ourselves to grieve, it is also crucial that we work through to letting go and moving on. It's just possible that in some cases what we are holding on to is keeping us from new and better things that God has for us.

6. King of the Castle?

Submission. Ewwww, there's that "S" word! I used to absolutely *hate* to hear anyone teach on the subject or even bring it up in conversation—unless I could put in my two cents worth! I had all the usual arguments in my arsenal to defend my lack of the quality! For example, 1) women aren't meant to be doormats; 2) the Scripture teaches that believers are supposed to submit to each *other*, not just the wife to the husband (Ephesians 5:21); 3) if Tracy would do his part to love me and lead our family, I'd find it easy to submit; 4) even God Himself used women in the Bible to lead others (Deborah, for example); and 5) you can't follow if nobody is leading! But the truth was, it was a touchy subject to me, probably because I had such great need in this area. I was living far from the truth of God's Word, and it took years for the Lord to get me to a place where I would even hear it.

Thankfully, though, the Lord is patient and willing to keep speaking to us in a certain area until we're ready to hear. In fact, He sometimes gets very quiet about everything else until we see that we need to start listening more closely! In my case, I had to work past my need for Gene's affection and the issues involved there. Then as the Lord began to show me what a controlling person I was, He let me know there was help available if I would open myself to Him and His Word. Since I was ready to hear, He led me to a book by Genevieve White titled *Daughters of Sarah*.

I was totally shocked to learn that God's order for the family really *is* for the husband to lead the family, regardless of the gifts of the wife. I grew up during the 60's and 70's when women's lib was affecting every specter of American society. I had bought into some of the ideas about women needing to stand up for their rights. I picked up the chant that women are not doormats, and even though I was a believer, I hadn't been taught what the Bible had to say about the roles of men and women. Even when I gave my life to the Lord and got serious about following Him and studying His Word, I still didn't see the truth of His plan—even after reading the Bible MANY times over. Somehow the verses with these truths just slipped past me or went over my head.

But I learned that God isn't against women; Jesus gave women more dignity than they'd ever been shown in history! In fact, those who believe that the concept of submission puts women in a subservient role that is degrading should take a good look at the lesson history has for us. Every society that has embraced Christianity and all its teachings has seen wondrous opportunities for women! Jesus taught that women should be loved with the utmost—loved as He loves the church, giving His life for her! God is not against women, and neither are the teachings of the Bible.

Although husbands and wives are to have submissive attitudes towards one another and cooperate with each other, the final decision maker is meant to be the husband. After all, he is the one who will stand before God to give an account for what happened in the family! Probably what was most shocking about this revelation was that I learned that living a life of submission was actually what I'd been looking for all along! God didn't want me to be a doormat, but neither did He want me stressed out all the time trying to fulfill a role I wasn't designed to function in!

I began to realize that even when God used women to lead men in Scriptural examples, it was often because the man He had called to do the job simply refused to do it. In Deborah's case, she warned the man that the glory would go to a woman since he wasn't courageous enough to stand up and take his place in leading Israel into battle! Of course, He used many other women, and He has continued to do so through the ages, but the pattern for the home is clearly outlined in Scripture, and that's one place the man is supposed to lead.

I also could see that my complaints about Tracy not loving me the way I needed him to were partially my own fault. And the main reason Tracy wasn't going anywhere for me to follow was because I didn't give him a chance to lead. He'd given up much earlier in our marriage because it just wasn't worth fighting me for the position.

So I was starting to see what submission was *not*; next I needed to discover what submission really *is*. It is yielding to the power, control, or authority of another person. It is the opposite of what I'd done all my life; I had refused to yield to anyone else totally, because I didn't trust anyone, especially not men! To my amazement and great relief, I found that I could trust the Lord to love me enough to protect me. I didn't have to hold the power. I didn't have to control situations and people. I could enjoy relaxing in the decisions of someone else in authority, in this case, my husband.

Changing my way of interacting with Tracy didn't happen overnight, though. Neither did it mean I quit having opinions. It didn't mean that I ceased sharing my insights with him, either, but the way I communicated gradually did a 180° turn! As I began to walk in the truth in this area, I found it freeing just to share my opinion then let go of the outcome! From things as trivial as choosing a restaurant to important decisions such as what vehicle to purchase, I began to find new depths of trusting the Lord than I'd ever imagined possible! I was learning that God truly is able to lead our family through my husband! I found that Tracy had talents and abilities that had been hidden to me before, and it was exciting to see leadership qualities growing in him.

I also began to see that my attitude was where the battle was waged; instead of having a critical spirit towards Tracy and all he did, I needed to reverence him. That can be summed up quite simply in these words: "I think you are a very neat guy!" As I gave up control and trusted in Jesus, I was freed to see what a neat guy Tracy really is!

The growth has been steady through the years, and as long as I keep the truth in front of me, I move in that direction. In fact, as part of my daily devotions, I read a portion of Genevieve's book after my regular Bible reading just to keep my rebellious nature in check! I quickly go back to my manipulative ways unless I keep reading the truth to wash my thought life clean and help keep my motives pure. But I have forty plus years of "stinking thinking" to reprogram, so there are still challenges from time to time!

I don't think we can get to the place where we can consider ourselves submissive wives, any more than we can get to the place where we can consider ourselves "good" Christians. It is a walk, a journey, a changing from one degree of glory to the next. We will have good days and bad, and we will sometimes think it's one step forward, two steps back! But the important thing is to keep walking! Don't quit or give up! Realize it is Jesus Who works in us, both to will and to do His good pleasure. If we are willing, He will continue to teach us and give us grace!

It is so easy to judge other people by what we see on the outside. The funny thing is, we usually base our appraisal of someone's submission on her personality instead of actual yieldedness. Sometimes the quiet women are the most rebellious! They might not fuss and fight with their husbands or ever contradict them in public, but they might use the silent treatment or manipulate in more subtle ways! The Lord is looking at the heart, and He knows how to judge the intents He finds there. He even knows when we are outwardly yielding, but still holding on to control and trying to get what we want through the supposed submission! Nothing gets past His all-seeing eyes!

But *we* need to withhold judgment of others as much as possible. It always gets us into trouble! I've noticed a tendency in the body of Christ in recent years to assume that if someone is having serious problems or sin issues, then that person probably wasn't saved to begin with. Tidy! Takes care of any loose ends we have in our thinking! But Christians have "issues"! Salvation does NOT equal sanctification! True, positionally we are made holy and complete when we accept Jesus as our Savior! When God looks at us after we receive Jesus, He doesn't see our sin; He sees the blood of His Son covering us!

But the Bible tells us to work out our own salvation, too! (Phil. 2:12) Getting that wonderful healing of spirit and soul into our daily lives is a lifelong process! Any of us who has been saved for any length of time knows that it doesn't happen overnight!

Neither does salvation equal maturity! Think about it: if a baby poops in his pants, you don't say he must not be a human! It's just what babies do! But if he's still pooping in his pants at thirty years old, then there's a problem! He's still a human being, but he's not functioning properly! He didn't mature like he was supposed to! The same is true in the spirit. Someone might be born again yet never have completed the necessary training to grow as a child of God. So many things block our growth. We have an enemy, Satan, who wants to destroy us! In fact, his main job is to steal, kill, and destroy us (John 10:10)! He is jealous of our position with the Lord God! If he can't have us for eternity, he sure wants to make certain that we won't be able to take anyone else with us to heaven! He wants to make us ineffective.

Thank the dear Lord, we DO have a way to fight against Satan's devices! But don't assume that problems or sin equate to a lack of salvation. The Word is clear: anyone who confesses that Jesus is Lord and that God raised Him from the dead will be saved! (Romans 10:9) It is easy to be saved! Just not as easy to work out that salvation! We need to PRAY for those who are struggling instead of judging them and writing them off!

And we need to be sure to give ourselves grace while we're at it. It is not healthy to compare ourselves with others. We will either begin to think there is no hope for us because we are SO far behind those we're watching, or we'll start thinking more highly of ourselves than we ought to!

We also need to consider where we started on this journey of living the Christian life. If a person were raised in a Christian home, he might be further along morally when starting the journey. He is probably going to appear to have his life more figured out and holy than someone who knew nothing about Christianity, who might have come from a terribly dysfunctional family background. That kind of person might seem to be doing worse than the first example even after ten years of being a Christian! Truth told, though, that "heathen" might actually have grown WAY more than the morally solid person and could have actually made more progress! Let me give an example to make it more clear: the moral person might have NO bad habits yet be full of self-righteousness and self-centeredness and a critical spirit and be quite content to stay that way. The morally deficient person might still smoke and occasionally swear but could have already given up drugs and alcohol and illicit sex! This one might be tender towards the Lord, humble, willing to change, and making great strides towards becoming more like Jesus even though there is still a bad habit or two!

You might see where I am and think, "What a mess!" But you don't know what I WAS! I know how far God has brought me! We come into the Kingdom at various stages of morality, understanding, background, etc. He takes us where we are! "Just as I am" seems fine for salvation and a Billy Graham crusade, but we expect each other to be perfect immediately following the conversion! Or at least as perfect as WE are! We're being changed one day at a time—and not always on the time schedule we prefer. Whoever thinks he is "finished" just doesn't see his own wretchedness clearly! Oswald Chambers had a true grasp of our sinfulness. This reading is taken from June 21 in his collection *My Utmost for His Highest.*

> *How long is it going to take God to free us from the morbid habit of thinking about ourselves? We must get sick unto death of ourselves, until there is no longer any surprise at anything God can tell us about ourselves. We cannot touch the depths of meanness in ourselves. There is only one place where we are right, and that is in Christ Jesus.*

Needing Jesus certainly applies when we begin to give up the lordship of our lives and move towards living a life of submission and abandonment to the Lord and our husbands. If there were a fail-proof formula for being a submissive wife, none of us would need Jesus in this important area of life! Sometimes we tend to think of the Ten Commandments as ten steps towards righteous living, but the truth is, we can't (and don't) keep those, either—at least not perfectly in our hearts. We never reach a plateau where we can decide we've arrived and can stop growing. Sure enough, as soon as we begin to think we've really made it, the Lord is faithful to show us another area where we truly need His salvation from self! We don't even KNOW how much junk is in us! The process is as important as the destination in the Christian walk, and the same is true in submission. It's all about yielding more of ourselves to the Lord, trusting that He loves us and wants good for us.

Jesus doesn't reform our human natures; He asks us to crucify them so He can live in and through us! I can't change myself or be good enough to please God! I need Jesus, and so do you! He is able, though, and will do wonders in us if we are willing! Still, it does take willingness. Oswald Chambers (July 8 selection) says that we must *exercise* our wills rather than giving them up! It is so easy to lie back lamely, expecting God to change us, but He won't unless we are actively willing to change in a particular area. Are we willing to read, listen to good teaching, make ourselves accountable in a certain area until the change comes?

You might be thinking that if you were married to a man like my husband, then it would be easy for you to be the kind of wife you need to be, and you'd be content. Well, I can promise you that my husband is no different from yours! We have had to deal with HUGE sin issues! There has had to be lots of forgiveness, and we've let go of many shattered dreams. If your husband is not a Christian, then that *is* a different situation, but remember that Christians are also still human beings with the potential to fall short—way short! Tracy has done horrible things, and so have I! But following God's plan for the family is still the best plan! It's our only hope! The results are not disappointing, either!

Don't despise small beginnings. You might not get off to a galloping start, but as you trust in the Lord and keep taking another step, He will do something by His Spirit. You have to start somewhere, and He takes you as you are! It isn't about how fast you get there, because remember, it isn't about reaching a destination! It's the journey that makes the difference! You are making progress as long as you are putting one foot in front of the other, heading in the right direction!

If He is walking in and through us, then it's really a matter of making a place in us for Him to do so. John the Baptist came as a "voice of one calling in the desert, 'Prepare the way for the Lord, make straight paths for him.'" (Matthew 3:3) We still need to make a place ready for Him to walk, but it is no longer on natural roads; it is within us! We can make a place for Him inside us, where He is not only revered and worshipped, but also where He can walk and have free reign. We start out as a simple temple for the Holy Spirit, and He grows us into a cathedral! At times we will be clinging tightly to what we want, and it will take all we have in us to relinquish our own desires, but it only takes *one* move towards the Lord, and He comes running to our aid!

Neglecting this truth can have repercussions for years. One of my shortfalls is pushing for something to happen NOW instead of waiting on the Lord and waiting on Tracy. A few years ago, we needed new transportation desperately. Our van had finally "given up the ghost," and we didn't have the money to buy another vehicle AND keep sending our children to Central Christian School, where we felt they belonged. A friend of mine asked me if we'd talked to the area churches about helping us out. She felt that with our adopted children and huge family, perhaps other believers would want to pitch in. I was surprised by that suggestion, and although it went against my grain, I went ahead and wrote a letter to ten churches in the area. We received a little help towards a vehicle; then someone helped tremendously with our tuition for the children's schooling.

I didn't give it any more thought for a long time, until during the fall of 2000. I was scheduled to speak and sing at a church not too far from home, and it was one of the ten churches I had mailed the letter to, asking for them to consider helping with our transportation. The pastor of the church told me that when he had received that letter, he had thrown it in the trash! Why? Because *I* had been the one to write it instead of my husband doing so! Back in those days when the letter was written, I not only paid the bills, but I also was in charge of all the decision-making concerning our finances. It was a major area of control in our marriage, and even though part of me wanted Tracy to take leadership, I also had a part that enjoyed having the power that came with deciding how the money was spent. I didn't even ask Tracy about sending that letter! Even years later, it was still having an effect on my effectiveness in ministry, because the pastor of that church wasn't even sure he wanted me to speak to the women! I ended up going, because the pastor and his wife called and visited with me and received my permission to talk to my pastors for a recommendation, and the Lord blessed the time spent at his church. But I had let my rebellious, independent spirit harm both my witness and others' opinions of my husband. My motive was not to harm his reputation, but that was still the end result.

Am I saying that the husband has to pay the bills? Am I saying a woman is rebellious if she has that duty? No! I'm saying that's how it was at my house! It wasn't just that I paid the bills—it was also that I enjoyed the power and control it gave me, and I didn't even consult my husband before taking our problems to others. Even if I had, at that time in our lives, he probably wouldn't have disagreed with me, simply because it was too much work to do so!

Often, the damage caused by fighting our husbands on an issue can be worse than the results of what we are disagreeing about. Let me explain. We have some friends who have adopted some children. The oldest is a girl, and she is at the age where she wants to wear makeup like her friends do. Her dad wants to let her, knowing the young lady already feels "different" from the other children because she's adopted. The mother, however, simply won't stand for it. She has put her foot down on the makeup issue; she doesn't wear much makeup herself, and she doesn't want the girl to grow up too early. Yet resisting her husband will have a far worse effect on the daughter than the makeup ever could. She is teaching her daughter rebellion—the very thing she wants to avoid for her daughter! Her heart's desire for the girl is a good thing, but her method of getting it is not. How much better it would be to let her husband make the decision for their family, trusting God is big enough to care for their daughter through her husband. This would set an example of submission and love rather than rebellion, stubbornness, and pride. Her stand could very well come back to bite her in the end. I have certainly seen the exact same rebellious look in some of my kids' faces and heard the disrespectful tone in their voices that *I* showed their father in front of them! How sad!

How many of us know women who believe their crosses to bear are their husbands? Maybe we *are* women like that! Jesus isn't asking us to be martyrs in that sense! He does ask us to die daily—taking up our crosses to follow Him. He says that if we want to reign with Him, we must also suffer with Him. But it's the "with Him" that makes all the difference! It is only through death that we find life; it is only through giving up that we receive. If we try to hold on to this life and keep it or take what we think will bless us or make us happy, we will lose it. But if we willingly give up our rights and follow Jesus, we will find contentment.

The Lord wanted to teach me these concepts many years ago when Benjamin was a tiny baby. I took a class called "Eve Reborn," led by a dear friend, Gloria Levesque. I missed a lot of the concepts, even though I was present at the meetings, simply because I wasn't ready to hear them. I was SO FAR from being a woman of virtue who could reverence her husband, that I simply couldn't grasp many of the teachings. One thing that has stayed with me through the years, though, is the concept of "need versus need." It is the idea that each spouse wants his own needs met first. "If he would love me, then I would respect him," thinks the wife, while the husband is thinking, "If she'd respect me, it would be easy to love her." That is conditional love and respect; God wants us to serve one another in love with no strings attached. That's what Jesus did for us at the cross. He gave His life for all mankind, knowing that not all would receive His precious gift of salvation. We need to give our lives to our spouses as we promised to do when we entered into the marriage covenant.

The *Eve Reborn* teaching also exposed the "strange woman," who is the "other" woman that so often comes into a man's life. She ends up being a helper to him when the wife isn't. She even protects him from his wife! She often becomes a good sex partner and is the perfect counterfeit to God's plan for the man. She uses flattery in place of reverence, and he is fooled. The sad thing is, the wife actually invites that strange woman in when she withdraws reverence from her husband! This never excuses the man for sin, and he will still have to answer to God for his thoughts and actions, but we women can't ignore the part we play. The only way for a counterfeit to be exposed is for the wife to show the real thing!

I must remember that I submit to Tracy as unto the Lord because it's being obedient to Him—not so we'll have a better marriage, even though we *will* have a better marriage! I am to be obedient when Tracy's nice, when he's cranky, when he's leading, when he's neglecting his duties—I do it because it's right. And it's not a bargaining tool to try to get God to change Tracy! Our husbands will make mistakes and be selfish and tired or be guilty of having impure motives sometimes; they're human! We must not treat submission like a yo-yo—up if our husbands are being good and down if we think our husbands are falling short.

Which adjectives describe me? Nagging, quarrelsome, fault-finding, contentious, vexing, disagreeing, scolding, having many words, OR respectful, reverent, attentive, preferring him, venerating and esteeming him, deferring to him, full of praise for him, loving, and exceedingly admiring him? Yikes! Change me, Lord! I can't use tiredness or busyness or distractions or anything else as an excuse!

I have to consider what I do and say to either build Tracy up or tear him down. How much am I letting him know how he pleases and blesses me? Proverbs 14:1 tells us that the foolish woman tears down her house with her own hands, while the wise woman builds hers. It's not talking about physically getting mortar and stones and erecting the structure of the home; it's referring to the spirit of her home! We need to realize what impact we have on our husbands, children, and societies!

If we were perfect, we could cast the first stone! We need to give these men grace and know that it isn't our place to correct them or point out their faults to them. Whose place is it to make sure our husbands are walking with God or being obedient to His Word or even loving us properly? It's the Lord's! We are NOT the Holy Spirit! Is God big enough to lead these men? Yes! And we will be more help to Him by simply loving our husbands and building them up than by pointing out their faults to them! Would we want a perpetual list of our own faults? Would that encourage us to keep trying? Of course not! We actually end up delaying the work of God when we meddle.

God says in Hebrews 8 that He *forgets* the *bad* things we do; in Nehemiah 13, He tells us He also *remembers* the *good* things we do! We are supposed to treat each other the same way!

Most men already feel enough pressure in their God-given position. They often have very little confidence because for decades they have been made to look stupid and incapable! The media has patterned a disrespectful attitude towards bumbling, ineffective husbands and fathers, and we have bought into it. Men are already fighting an image of failure. We can make a huge difference for them when we quit fighting them on everything and start letting them learn, even if they have to learn by making mistakes sometimes!

It is easy to think that if our husbands would just do a better job of leading, we'd do a better job of submitting! It's true that when they are loving in their roles as leaders, seeking to serve their families through leading, it is easier to swallow our pride and accept their guidance! Isaiah 16:5 says, "In love a throne will be established. . . . " When a leader rules with love, there is no reason to rebel! If we know the leader has our best interest at heart, we trust him and eagerly look to him!

But what if our husbands are not Christians? What if they are saved, but they are cranky and hateful? What if they are not natural leaders? What if they don't want the job? What if they are surly and pompous and harsh? It doesn't change the truth! Nor does it change the freedom and peace we will find if we will still do what we are designed to do in marriage by finding our God-given roles!

If a man is not a Christian, it doesn't mean his wife doesn't have to obey God's Word on this topic. If he has accepted the Lord, yet isn't walking closely with Him, that doesn't negate God's commands to her, either. I love what Genevieve White teaches on this, and I strongly recommend that any woman who finds herself in this kind of situation read Genevieve's book for more understanding. The bottom line is, God put them in authority in the home. It's their position, just like someone having the position of bank president or school superintendent. It's a role they fill regardless of how well qualified we think they are! And that role comes with the parallel expectation of a certain degree of honor and respect.

Ecclesiastes 4 teaches us that two are better than one, but a cord of three strands is even better—it's not easily broken. Pray for your husband, not out of selfish motives, but because it is in agreement with God's Word! He wants our families healthy and whole and strong! But until you begin to see that happening, lovingly submit to your husband anyway. You will be amazed at the freedom you experience!

I must address one area that truly concerns me, because I know that women who are being abused might have a skewed notion of what submission is. I just don't know how to word it any more plainly than this: if your husband (or boyfriend, which is even more common) is knocking your around, beating you, hitting you, slapping you, pushing you, or doing anything else that physically puts you in danger, your putting up with it is NOT biblical submission! Staying in a dangerous position is NOT biblical submission! Keeping your children in a position to be harmed is NOT biblical submission! It is neediness instead! It is saying that you need this person or that he needs you, even though he is mean and disrespectful to you and endangering your life or that of your children—or both.

If you stay in a situation like that, you are basically telling God that He is not enough for you or that you are not worthy of the good He has planned for you. Neither is true! *RUN*, DO NOT *WALK*, TO GET *HELP*! You are worth FAR more than the treatment you are receiving! You can maintain a submissive *attitude* that says that you respect your husband's position as head of the family and that you will not be hateful or disdain him. Communicate that you will not put him down to the children. But neither will you allow harm to come to yourself or your children! There is help available for men who want it, and you simply must not endanger yourself or others in a way that really only enables the man to continue a behavior that deep down, he doesn't want, either.

For the majority of us, though, our biggest problem is our own selfish will. My job is not to correct, teach, or judge my husband. It is to love and respect him. As I pray for him and accept him, I am freed to see what God can do. When I fail to live up to what I know in this area, I ask the Lord to forgive me. Then I go to Tracy to ask for his forgiveness. When I take too long to work through it, our home is full of tension. During a time of great stress when I was on birth control pills (to regulate my hormones, not to prevent pregnancy!) and trying to make our Christmas celebration special to our family, I got focused on my own needs and really blew up at Tracy. The next day I was repentant, and I was sure to apologize to him and find out what he needed that night.

He was SO sweet! He held me in his lap for a long time (unusual—he usually only does this for a few minutes because it makes his legs hurt!), then even started pretending to be Santa, complete with ho-ho-ho-ing and asking me what I wanted for Christmas. He had all of us cracking up totally! What a guy! And what a God we serve! Tracy took something that was hard and wrong and helped turn it into a fun memory for all of us! Thank You, Jesus!

Is it always easy to submit? No! If that were true, it probably wouldn't even be real submission—we'd just be at peace because we were getting our way! But the fruit of true submission from the heart is worth the sacrifices made!

If we will just lay down the reins of control, we'll begin to feel more like queens in our homes. We'll enjoy the peace that God meant for us to have in our supportive role as wives. God is waiting to prove to you how big He is and how much He loves you! Just give the control of your life—all of it—to Him!

7. There Are Dragons Out There!

It is one thing to know hypothetically that there are dragons outside the safety of the castle walls, but it is quite another thing to have been personally burned by dragon's breath! When you have already been scorched, you tend to want to stay away from the windows where you might see even the hint of smoke! At least for a while, anyway, until the burns begin to heal.

In fact, it can be easy to completely give up when we've been hurt badly. It is human nature for us to try to protect ourselves. That's why we instinctively blink and draw back when we see something being thrown toward us. We can watch toddlers who have been burned by hot food or a stove of some type—one of the first words they seem to learn is "hot." Pain is quite a teacher, and we learn early on to avoid the physical kind whenever possible.

When we have been hurt in our marriages, we tend to withdraw, too. Maybe you've seen counselors, read books, and attended marriage encounters, but nothing has changed. You have let your hopes rise, only to be disappointed time after time. Maybe after trying for so many years, all to no avail, you feel it would be much easier to just leave things as they are. Getting your hopes up for things to be better might take more courage, energy, and grace than you think you are willing to give right now.

Let me share about a time when I was ready to give up in another area. In July, 1994, when my sister Cathy gave birth to Rebekah, I had already suffered six of my ten miscarriages. I was facing a decision about whether or not to have my doctor do some more testing to see why I lost babies so easily. I was already in tremendous emotional pain, because I had been due to deliver just three days from Rebekah's due date, but we had lost that baby. Although Tracy and the children and I rejoiced with Cathy and her family for their precious blessing, I still didn't know whether or not to move forward with the testing my doctor was recommending. Did I want to hope for an answer to the miscarriages or just remain as we were so I wouldn't have to face disappointment?

I ended up proceeding with testing, and as it turned out, I was low on progesterone. Eventually, we were able to add Anna Marie to our family, and she has brought more joy than we thought possible. She blessed all nine of the rest of us, and we doted on her! It took courage, though, and making ourselves vulnerable to more potential pain.

The Word of God is reliable. Romans 5:2-5 tells us that the hard things we go through can eventually lead to hope if the Lord is involved in our lives.

> *And we rejoice in the hope of the glory of God. Not only so, but we also rejoice in our sufferings, because we know that suffering produces perseverance; perseverance, character; and character, hope. And hope does not disappoint us, because God has poured our His love into our hearts by the Holy Spirit, Whom He has given us.*

If we are hoping that a man will fulfill us totally and make us happy, then we will be sadly disappointed! That kind of happiness is always temporary! But if we are hoping in the Lord, seeking to be a vessel for Him to pour love through, then we have reason to smile! The Lord does NOT disappoint us! He fills us to overflowing if we look to Him!

It is true that after my tenth miscarriage, I wasn't very hopeful. Tracy convinced me to just try ONE more time, and that was the time we got our Anna. Sometimes it's that one more time that makes all the difference. Identifying the source of the problem with my miscarriages—low progesterone—was the second step towards our answer. The first was being willing to be tested. In your marriage, God is looking for willingness. He does NOT want to hurt you! He wants to help. Once you really give it to Him and open your heart, He can help you define the core issues or problems that are keeping you from moving forward successfully. (No, the problem is NOT just your husband!)

The Lord wants us to have healthy, whole families, and they start with the marriage relationship. If we approach our marriages with the desire to be obedient to the Lord and grow closer to Him, then that attitude will help us press forward during the tough times. Trying to see what we can get out of the relationship will lead to disappointment and grief; looking to Jesus, Who loves us, will birth new hope in our hearts. We can trust Him!

We read in Matthew 3:11 that Jesus came to baptize us with the Holy Spirit and fire. The Holy Spirit is likened to wind in the Bible, and when we surrender to Jesus, His Spirit becomes a driving force in our lives. The storms that come with high winds and waves can threaten to shipwreck us if we forget about Him! But wind can accomplish some very good things, too. It blows the dead leaves off of trees, and all of us have some "dead stuff" that needs to be blown away. Wind also blows seeds to fertile ground, where something new can start to grow. We need Him to blow in seeds of life that are required to grow something worthwhile in us. Jesus spoke peace to the wind and waves of storms, and they were still. He will speak peace to the storms of life we are facing, too. Then we can ask His Spirit to blow in and through our lives, and He will bring the good things that only wind can bring.

Jesus also baptizes us with fire. Fire is a cleanser; the heat sterilizes and draws out impurities. It destroys debris—perhaps what was churned up with the wind! He simply won't let the heat get turned up too high. He is the Master of the fire.

Several dear friends have forwarded me a message about the refining of silver; I regret that I don't know where it originally came from, so I can't give credit to the author. It is so powerful, though, that I want to share it with you here. Remember, the pain is not meant to destroy us; rather, it can be used to help and change us, sending us to the One Who can really make a difference. Here is the story:

> *Malachi 3:3 says, "He will sit as a refiner and purifier of silver."*
>
> *This verse puzzled some women in a Bible study, and they wondered what this statement meant about the character and nature of God. One of the women offered to find out the process of refining silver and get back to the group at their next Bible study.*
>
> *That week, the woman called a silversmith and made an appointment to watch him at work. She didn't mention anything about the reason for her interest beyond her curiosity about the process of refining silver.*
>
> *As she watched the silversmith, he held a piece of silver over the fire and let it heat up. He explained that in refining silver, one needed to hold the silver in the middle of the fire where the flames were hottest to burn away all the impurities. The woman thought about God holding us in such a hot spot, then she thought again about the verse that says, "He sits as a refiner and purifier of silver." She asked the silversmith if it was true that he had to sit there in front of the fire the whole time the silver was being refined.*
>
> *The man answered that yes, he not only had to sit there holding the silver, but he had to keep his eyes on the silver the entire time it was in the fire. If the silver was left a moment too long in the flames, it would be destroyed.*

The woman was silent for a moment. Then she asked the silversmith, "How do you know when the silver is fully refined?"

He smiled at her and answered, "Oh, that's easy—when I see my image in it."

If today you are feeling the heat of the fire, remember that God has His eye on you and will keep watching you until He sees His image in you.

Now it's true that the world will knock us around and we'll get burned sometimes—no doubt about it! In fact, it isn't just the world that we face—we have three enemies that seek our harm. The world, the flesh, and the devil are against the Lord and His ways in our lives. If there are enemies, then that must mean there is a battle to fight. And after all, didn't Prince Charming fight the dragon for his princess?

The world seeks our destruction by enticing us. If we can be persuaded to commit sin, that's a victory for the world. If not, then a sin of omission will work just as well—just simply being so busy that we can't stay focused on what is important. The world refers to the entire system this earth functions under. Jesus said that friendship with the world is enmity with God! We don't want to get caught up in what the world says is right, acceptable, pleasing, or good. The world today has launched a major attack on the family! Stable homes with a godly, responsible father, a mother who has put her family before her career, and obedient children are mocked through the media and politics!

The flesh, or our sinful nature, strives against the Spirit's wishes at all times! Sin is progressive and is never satisfied! When it is fed, it craves more, rather than getting "full." When we read, view, and think about things that are contrary to God's Word, our flesh is strengthened and our spirits lag. The same is true when we spend our free time with those of questionable character. The Proverbs tell us that bad company corrupts good morals. That bad company isn't always another person in today's world; it can come through movies, magazines, novels, soap operas, and so on!

Our flesh and the world work together to ensnare us. Think of the story of Lot; it is found in Genesis, chapters 13 and 19. He gradually got into the wicked city of Sodom, but eventually, it also got into him! First he pitched his tent near Sodom. Then he moved in. Then he wanted to sit in the city gate, where the spiritual authority of the city was. When the Lord decided to destroy this wicked city, and Lot and his family were fleeing for their lives, his wife's heart was still in Sodom, so she turned back and was paralyzed as she turned to a pillar of salt, finally unable to move forward.

How often sin is like that! We get desensitized to the effects of the world when we allow the media and attitudes around us to come in. We don't need friendship with the world; we need Christian friends!

Think, too, of Sampson. He loved Delilah, so much so that even when she betrayed him, he didn't get away from her! He should have left her the first time she betrayed him, but he stayed for her to do it again and again. The third time, he actually told her the real secret of his strength, and she was his undoing. Some of the saddest words in the Bible are found in Judges 16:20. "But he did not know that the Lord had left him." Sampson thought he would be able to arise and conquer the Philistines if Delilah called them to cut his hair. But he was so out of touch by then, he didn't even realize his danger or that his strength was gone.

Jesus promised never to leave us or forsake us (Hebrews 13:5)! But certainly our strength can wane, and we can be in a state where we aren't *aware* of His presence. Thankfully, just as Sampson was able to re-grow his hair and perform the greatest feat of his life afterwards, we can also make our way back to the Lord. But at what price? His was blindness and death. We know that we will also pay a price when we get so far away that we don't even know where we are with the Lord.

Of course, the third enemy is Satan himself. He hates God, he hates Christians, and he hates families. He hates the freedoms we have in America. If he can ruin our marriages, he will then ruin families and our entire society in America. He will also deter our ability to reach other people for the Lord.

Often we are unaware that the devil is REAL, and he even has people who serve him! Satanists usually have "curse" lists with the names of Christian leaders on them. They work to bring down those who are having an effect on the lives of other people! My Uncle Bobby and Aunt Mary are officers in the Salvation Army. When they were pastoring in West Virginia, they kept having trouble with the church van. As they would go over a mountain, the headlights would quit working! This happened repeatedly, and the mechanic could never find anything wrong. Finally they learned that an actual witch was attending their services! They took the matter to the Lord, equipped with an understanding of how Satan works, and once they had bound the enemy, the van immediately stopped having the problem with the lights!

Satan has at his disposal one third of the heavenly host—those former angels that rebelled against God and are now the demonic forces that plague the earth's inhabitants. When Tracy and I first got married, he would fall asleep quickly while I lay for quite awhile waiting for sleep to come. One night, I suddenly became quite fearful. I realized that a demon spirit of fear was in our bedroom. I was petrified and laid shivering while waiting for it to leave or for sleep to finally overtake me. After putting up with a repeat performance of this for several nights, I finally got bold enough to do something about it! Trembling, I began to sing a praise chorus, "Praise Thy holy Name, Lord, praise Thy holy Name; it's a mighty tower, praise Thy holy Name. The righteous run into it to hide them from the storm! Praise Thy holy Name, Lord, praise Thy holy Name." That demon left long before the song was over, and it NEVER came back! God says He inhabits the praises of His people, and demons REALLY don't like to be in His presence!

We don't have to go looking for demons behind every bush to find evidence of Satan's work, though! He is much more crafty than we think! Seldom do we see him in the "Exorcist" type of display with heads turning 180° or people puking green stuff! He is far subtler than that under normal circumstances! In fact, C.S. Lewis showed us Satan's most common tactic in his classic *The Screwtape Letters*. In this book, the devil assigns a demon the job of causing a particular human being to fall. The demon is delighted to learn that he doesn't have to do much at all! If he can just get the man to fuss with those around him, the job is almost done! The enemy knows that if he can keep us at odds with each other, we'll be of no value in fighting spiritual warfare or reaching anyone else for the Kingdom of God! This is particularly true in marriage!

You might wonder what all this talk of fighting is about! Isn't Christianity supposed to be a peaceful religion? Yes and no! We do receive great peace, because Jesus is the Prince of Peace! He also gives us peace that passes understanding—a sense of calm and trust and faith even when all hell is breaking loose around us! Peace in our souls when circumstances scream that we ought to be falling apart! And most importantly, we receive peace with God. But there is also a battle waging in the spiritual realm.

> *January 22, 1987 There is a fight to be fought in the kingdom of God—in our individual lives as well as collectively. If we don't fight (unwilling, unskilled, afraid, unaware, unable, etc.), then we'll be overtaken. It's*

foolish to "strike up deals" with the enemy—he strips you blind, takes your wealth, your treasure—leaves you barren.

It's much better to ***fight****—Matthew 11:12 says, ". . . the kingdom of God has been forcefully advancing, and forceful men lay hold of it."*

I think I'll "take" this day in the kingdom. Why be robbed? I have everything available to me to win the fight—truth, righteousness, going with the gospel of peace, faith, salvation, His Word, prayer in the Spirit.

How silly to think we don't want to be in bondage to the enemy, but we don't want to gird up and fight him, either. So we just pay him off, passively. We let him take the best of our lives and days. ENOUGH!

Thankfully, the Lord didn't leave us powerless or defenseless against our foes, either! He gave us powerful weapons with which to fight! We find them listed in Ephesians chapter 6.

We have the belt of truth buckled around our waists. This piece of armor is like a girdle that protects us where we are most vulnerable. The truth is powerful, and knowing the truth is a huge protection when the lies of the enemy attack us. We have the breastplate of righteousness. This doesn't mean we're perfect—far from it! But we have put our faith in the righteousness of God, and His goodness protects our hearts. Our feet have been fitted with the gospel of peace. Wherever we go, through the battle, the storm, or the fire, we have the assurance of God's peace that comes from understanding the Good News of the gospel! The helmet of salvation is our covering mentally; much of the battle we face takes place between our ears! Without being saved, we have already lost! But once we know Jesus and His saving power, then there is a barrier between Satan and our minds.

In addition to these pieces, we also have the shield of faith, which is a mighty weapon. It is the last of the protective weapons at our disposal. When the enemy throws his darts and lies at us, we don't even have to understand everything; if we just continue to trust in the Lord Jesus, fully relying on His love and goodness, those fiery darts won't penetrate! Even when we can't tell up from down, when all appears to be lost, faith protects us. Hebrews 11 tells us that faith is being sure of what we hope for and certain of what we can't see. It's knowing because we know because we KNOW that God is in control and has our good in mind.

For an offensive weapon with which to actually fight our enemy, we've been given the sword of the Spirit, which is God's Word! Hebrews 4:12 says that God's Word is living and active, that it is sharper than any double-edged sword. It tells us that the Word can penetrate through all the junk to let us see what is of God and what is of man—dividing soul and spirit. It reveals the thoughts and attitudes and motives of our hearts! It will have that effect on whatever the devil is throwing our way, too!

And above all, when we have girded ourselves up with all the armor, we are told to pray all kinds of prayers. Did you know there are different kinds? Prayer is talking to God, and we can tell Him how much we love Him, we can thank Him for all He's done, we can ask Him to guide us and help us, and we can pray for others who are hurting. We can tell Him how we're feeling, knowing He will truly understand. We can confess our sins and faults, knowing He will still love us. Remember, His Word is our sword and gives us the truth; it says there is nothing we can do to separate us from His love! (Romans 8:38-39)

If you feel as though you're getting beaten up time and time again, then take a look at your armor. It is something we choose to put on. First, are you saved? Have you ever invited Jesus into your life as your God and King? Being one of the redeemed doesn't mean troubles will leave, but it does give you a starting place for fighting the battles you will face! Next, are you feeding your spirit with the truth, digging into the Scriptures to find out what God has to say about life? Are you being fed His Word by a pastor who has studied the Scriptures, as well? Both of these activities will help you learn to wield your sword! How's your prayer life? Do you worry and stew and fret and only turn to the Lord when all else has failed? Thanks be to God, He still answers those prayers, but He longs to commune with us all the time, not just during our troubles.

When we pray, we are taking ground. The Lord gave mankind authority to rule over the earth back in the Garden of Eden. Satan got that authority by default, but when Jesus came to earth, He restored our authority! He got the keys of death and hell from Satan, and He redeemed us back to our original purpose on earth. Satan can only do what someone *lets* him do!

I know that popular Christian teaching says that everything happens for a "reason," meaning that it was God's will. I must disagree strongly! *Sin* is *never* His will! He *hates* it! He did give man free will, so in that regard, He allows it. But He wants what is good and righteous. He also never wants anyone to perish, yet people perish daily, headed straight for an eternity in hell! That's not His will, either! He sacrificed His precious Son so anyone who would believe could be saved!

Perhaps you've been hurt badly by someone else, and you wonder where God was when you were going through it. If you've been around this common Christian teaching, you might have been led to believe that God had a purpose and plan in your pain and that He wanted it to happen to you so that you could someday help others in the same situation. You might even distrust Him since He didn't stop the circumstances that brought you pain.

While it's true that He *can* and *does* somehow work good out of every situation for people who love Him and are called according to His purposes (Romans 8:28), Scripture is clear that He does not desire evil. Ever. Period. For people who are not His children, life does NOT work out for their good! Contrary to popular belief, it does NOT all come out in the wash!

And it's SO important to get this: when bad things happen, it is because of the free will He gave to all men! That free will does not apply only to the "good guys"! It was given to all. God doesn't step in and stop bad people from doing bad things if that is what they choose to do.

So do we have any hope? Are we at the mercy of anyone who comes along? Not necessarily! That would be forgetting about our weapons, particularly prayer! Follow me for a moment and open your heart to consider what I'm saying, especially if this is contrary to what you've been taught before!

The Deists, in the early years of our country's founding, believed that God created the world, then just let it go, much like winding up a watch and letting it wind down of its own volition. They believed that He wasn't intimately involved with mankind once creation was over. My reasoning does not match the Deist's way of thinking! Although He did give man a free will, and He is a gentleman Who won't barge in to make anyone do something against his will, He still responds to the prayers of His people! He still wants us to exercise dominion and authority over this earth! That's why the Word urges us to pray! If our prayers did nothing, why would we be required to utter them? He promises to hear and do what we ask of Him in faith!

Back when Anne was helping me run my day care, she had asked me to pray for her visit to the dentist. On my way home from class, I asked the Lord to help her get the dental work done without feeling any pain. I sensed the Holy Spirit asking me if I really believed He could do that. It shocked me! I knew He *could* but I really didn't think He *would*! So I prayed again, asking for forgiveness for my doubt, and then repeating my request for her, this time in faith! I told her what I'd prayed when I relieved her to leave the day care, and she returned with a wonderful report of NO PAIN! The Word tells us that God's eyes rove through the earth, searching for someone who believes. I want to be that one!

It has taken me a long time to understand how important prayer is and how much the Lord desires for us to use the power He has given us. Recently He showed me that I need to pray with the same expectation of results that I get and expect when I tell my children what to do! That is SO huge! I was reflecting on how hard it is for me to see parents with unruly children who won't obey them. I also hate to see a teacher with a classroom out of control. It goes beyond my ability to comprehend why they would allow that kind of environment. I just figure that we are bigger than the children, and we have the authority over them, so there is no question about who is in control. We have tools at our disposal to make them WANT to do what we tell them, if we will just apply the correct tools, whether we use a spanking, grounding, referral, detention, or whatever.

Well, the Lord showed me that when I pray, I need to expect exactly the same kinds of results! I need to expect that whatever I'm praying about must comply, just as I expect a child to comply with my wishes and instructions! He was teaching me that faith is like that! If I'm not expecting an answer to my prayers, there is no reason to bother uttering them! Faith is the substance of things hoped for, remember?

At first, it sounds like this is totally egotistical and that we are supposed to boss God around! Nothing could be further from the truth! Once we understand the position He has given us in the earth—one of authority—then we realize that the key is in finding out what HE wants done and praying that way!

Have you ever noticed how often we Christians just say, "Lord, Your will be done." We don't have a clue what His will is, and our past experience has told us that He probably won't do anything TOO dramatic, so we shouldn't stick our necks out too far in expectation. We play it safe and somewhat lazy, really! We think we can't know what He wants, but we CAN! He gave us sixty-six books put together into our Holy Bible, and they are crammed full of what He wants! When we read His Word, the handbook of His plan for us, and allow the Holy Spirit to guide us in prayer, we *can* know His will.

Romans 8:26-27 reads, "In the same way, the Spirit helps us in our weakness. We do not know what we ought to pray for, but the Spirit himself intercedes for us with groans that words cannot express. And he who searches our hearts knows the mind of the Spirit, because the Spirit intercedes for the saints in accordance with God's will." Many times when I have been confused or disheartened or at the end of my rope, I have just begun to let the Holy Spirit fill me with His presence. Slowly I begin to see the light and often actually gain understanding for how I should pray once He has comforted me and interceded for me so lovingly!

When God's Word tells us to pray for our leaders, there is a reason! They are on the front lines of battle, and we need to keep them lifted up. Haven't you ever wondered why children of ministers or godly people sometimes make such a mess of their lives? They are under HUGE attack! Not only can Satan mess up the kids' lives, but he can also get to the parents through their children. He's been practicing his schemes for about 6,000 years!

There is something to the idea of praying a hedge of protection around someone. We actually give angels the "right" to fight demonic spirits on our behalf when we pray! And remember that there are MORE good, holy angels than wicked demons! Two thirds of them stayed on the Lord's side!

When we read the verses about praying for our leaders, we usually think of government officials and pastors and our bosses at work, and that's all true. But what about our own husbands? Who else has the potential to affect our lives and those of our children more than these men? And if *we* aren't praying for them, who is? Is there any other person who would have as much vested interest in their well-being than we do? Perhaps their mothers pray for them, and we welcome that! And sometimes the Holy Spirit will impress a prayer warrior to lift them up in a particular situation. But when it gets down to the nitty-gritty of everyday life, it's just us wives who know their needs and weaknesses well enough to be current. We can be more effective than anyone else in lifting them up before the Father.

We do not want to be afraid of demons or the devil or evil! Proverbs 26:2 says, "Like a fluttering sparrow or a darting swallow, an undeserved curse does not come to rest." Amen! Even if we think we DO deserve it, because we've opened the door in some way to demons, we need to repent of that sin and plead the blood of Jesus over our own lives, homes, and families. The Lord came to help those who need help, and He will help us in these situations.

We have nothing to fear! God is stronger and bigger than the devil. In fact, years ago I remember being totally amazed when comparing the Lord with the devil. I used to think they were close to the same, with the devil just being a little bit lower than the Lord in power. But that is simply not the case! The devil is only a fallen angel, a creation of the Lord, NOT equal with God! And in Revelation we read that the day will come when we will narrowly consider the devil, looking at him and saying, "Is THIS the one who terrorized the nations?" [Capitals added!] He's SO much smaller than we give him credit for! Our Creator God is BIGGER than ANYTHING! And he loves us and wants to help us! He is on our side; we just need to get on His!

The Lord wants to protect us. When we think of a castle, we remember the moats that were built to keep the enemy out. Certainly it is easier to keep them out than it is to fight them once they've made their way in! If you have ever toyed with things that would be an open invitation to the devil or demons, you need to clean house! I'm talking about things like horoscopes, tarot cards, demonic games (board games or video/computer games), Harry Potter books and movies (or any others that teach witchcraft), holding seances, levitation, Ouija boards, new age teachings, meditation that empties your mind of thinking, and so on. These activities open the door to evil forces, and you need to get them out of your house and life! Ask the Lord to forgive you for looking to other powers instead of to Him. Pray that the blood of Jesus will cleanse you and your family and your house, and ask Him to replace all with His holy presence and love. Then put on your armor faithfully!

Some people find talk of the "blood of Jesus" offensive. But that is evidence of demons at work; they can't stand to hear about the blood of Jesus. Satan counterfeits the redeeming work of Jesus' blood by including the drinking of blood in rituals his followers engage in. The extent of their hatred for the blood of Jesus came home to me during a confrontation with one of my professors many years ago. I had been concerned about some things he was teaching in our psychology classes because some of the younger students seemed to be questioning their faith. I decided to go to him to give him a chance to explain himself. I tried to get him to tell me his definition of salvation, but he hedged and used familiar Christian terms without ever convincing me that he was talking about the same kind of salvation I know. He even said that the "salvation experience" he once had as a child held only historical significance to him presently. I finally decided to cut through the semantics and just get to the crux of the matter, so I asked him this: "Do you believe man is made good only by faith in the blood of Jesus?" This dignified, well-respected head of the psychology department jumped up out of his seat, towered over me menacingly and shouted at me, "Why does it have to be the blood? Why does it always have to be the blood?"

I had chills running up and down my spine while the hairs on my airs stood at attention! Our eyes locked, and I knew I was gazing at true evil. He got himself under control as I told him I was going to have to discuss our conversation with the dean of the college and the board. I have never forgotten his reaction, knowing it revealed exactly how Satan and his cohorts view the blood of Jesus. They know they will never experience God's saving grace, and they don't want us to, either! Plead that blood of Jesus over your entire family and trust Him to wash you clean!

So much of what the Lord tells us in His Word is for our protection! We tend to think He wants to spoil our fun, but it just isn't so! He created us, so He knows our needs far better than we do, and everything He's commanded us is to help us find contentment.

When Eve disobeyed God in the garden by eating the forbidden fruit, she was deceived. She thought God was withholding something good from her. She questioned His goodness and honesty, doubting His nature, thinking He was selfishly keeping the best position for Himself and not letting man in. Actually, God was protecting her and Adam. They already had the knowledge of good! All they had to gain from their disobedience was the knowledge of evil!

Even when the Lord banished them from the garden, He was protecting them, not just punishing them. He didn't want them to eat from the Tree of Life, thereby living forever in their sinful state. Eternal life needed to be given at a time when mankind could live forever in holiness, which is why He sent Jesus. He paid for our sins, allowing us to be restored to fellowship with God.

Part of realizing there are dragons out there is facing the need to do battle. We get SO lazy! When we are focused on our own needs, we forget that eternity is affected by what we do and say! Isn't that an amazing thing—that as small as we are, God still wants to use us to make a difference in eternity! Sometimes it's by leading someone to Him, sometimes it's by praying for others, sometimes it's by participating in some type of ministry, but we are meant to make a difference. It's one of the reasons He leaves us here after we accept His salvation!

Back in the summer of 2000, the Lord began teaching me more about His protection. At church, in teaching tapes, on the radio, etc—everything was speaking the same thing to me about hell's gates and the Lord's protection! We think of hell's gates as running after us when we read the Scripture that says "the gates of hell shall not prevail against us." But gates are to protect! They're defensive! Just like that moat around the castle—they keep someone out!

We are to go after *them*! The Lord doesn't give us armor to wear so that we can stay behind our gates and hide! We're to fight the enemy, clearly revealed to be Satan and his demons! We march against the gates of hell! They won't be able to prevail against us, so we can do it!

How do we do this practically? We find out what God has to say in whatever is warring on our thoughts and minds! We cast down imaginations and every high thing that exalts itself against knowing God! We find out what HE has to say on a matter, and exercise our faith in that! We memorize Scripture related to our particular battle, and we don't give up until we see an answer! The devil can't stand against that! Then we pray about it in the Spirit on all occasions with all kinds of prayers and requests! We need to put the devil on notice: he isn't going to win against *us*! We don't passively sit still and pray, hoping the devil won't tromp on us! We go after him, offensively!

I faced tremendous despair a few years ago when our daughter Jeri ran away from home. She had always struggled with making attachments with our family, and it seemed she was continuously in trouble. When she left, she ended up at the youth shelter and social services began their mandatory investigation to see if Jeri was considered a "child in need of care." Tracy and I had never felt equipped to deal with the issues Jeri brought into our home, and we knew we had failed her in many ways. But that didn't make the situation any less scary. We didn't know what was going to happen. Would social services take *all* of our children away while sorting through the circumstances? Would we be arrested? Would our lives fall apart?

One night during all the questions and fear, Tracy and I lay in bed talking. I was overcome with despair. My mind was running in circles, imagining all the possible outcomes awaiting us. Tracy finally realized that I had quit talking, and he asked me if I was okay. I couldn't even answer him; I was paralyzed emotionally. He began to pray but I couldn't join him. Finally I just called out, "Jesus!" Something broke in the spiritual realm and I was able to start praying. I told God how afraid I was and said that I felt I was standing on the edge of a precipice, and it was a SHORT step off the edge of it. I told Him I didn't know if I could even hold on.

The Lord immediately began to comfort me. He said that if I couldn't hold on, *He* would hold *me*. I felt as though He was wrapping His loving arms around me, and I was finally able to settle down and get some sleep. The war wasn't over in our situation but I had at least won a victory in that particular skirmish! Out of that painful time in our lives came one of the most powerful songs I've ever written, titled "The Coldest Winter." The chorus shouts, "And the coldest winter stung my eyes; it blew right through my soul, but it saved me a surprise. When the icy blast chilled my bones, the barren landscape made me cry; a seed fell to the ground and died; but hope was born and took away the sting: the coldest winter always turns to spring!"

Some time ago, a Christian organization that is very dear to our hearts was going through a major battle in the spirit. There had been much gossip and backbiting, false accusations, mean communications, untruths—things that were devouring the believers in leadership. A huge board meeting was coming up, and Tracy and I knew we needed to be there and that we needed to do battle in the spirit beforehand.

Naturally, the enemy was having a hay day with us in the days before the meeting! Tracy and I were tense with each other, irritated about little things and being sarcastic with each other. Our eyes were NOT on the Lord, nor were they on what He wanted to accomplish in and through us during this intense time of battle. Pride was keeping both of us from making up with each other and working through our disagreement! I would try to discuss it with him, but my arrogant attitude and insistence on being "right" kept Tracy from being willing to discuss our issues together. Finally, I wrote a note to Tracy, asking him to come to terms on it so we could be effective in the Kingdom's business. Here's a copy of the note I wrote.

Dear Tracy,

I know the enemy would love to drive a wedge between us. He doesn't have to try very hard when we have unresolved issues. I guess it's hard for me to understand WHY you won't get it all aired out—you don't want to face it or admit any wrongdoing. Is it because you don't want anything to change?

I don't know. But I do know that even though Satan likes discord ***any*** *time, he especially loves it when there's intense warfare already. If we're fussing or silent with each other, we can't "agree touching anything." We're rendered powerless to help fight. There's a huge* *board meeting tomorrow night, and monumental decisions being made . . . in the next few days. . . . For the sake of the Kingdom and the gospel, I want peace between us. I'm not saying all is well, because it isn't. But I* **am** *saying I want us to be united in battle. SO many people will be affected eternally by what is decided. Will you join me?*

Becky

He wrote a simple "yes" at the bottom of the note, and when he returned home from work that night, we were both freed to pray in unity and prepare spiritually for the meeting. God moved miraculously in the situation the ministry was facing, and Tracy and I were able to be effective during the battle.

I faced one of the most obvious attacks ever during the final rewrite of this book! Just in the three weeks I was editing it, here is how my family was afflicted: my brother-in-law Marvin punctured his lung, and the doctor didn't detect it for several days. He could have died! My mother had to be hospitalized to check for a possible heart attack. Thankfully she didn't have one, but we still don't know what is causing her symptoms. One of my nephews was hospitalized because he was feeling like committing suicide. My niece Candace was in a terrible car accident with her boyfriend and both had to be Care Watched to a hospital in Ft. Worth. Not to mention another niece running off and causing her parents great worry for several hours and some other issues with various kids in the family. One young person was so desperate, I took three days to research on the Internet, trying to find a solution for him.

Things happen to people every day, but you have to admit, this was quite a load for ONE family in just three short weeks! The enemy did NOT want me to finish this book in time for folks to give it for Christmas presents. He knew that if they couldn't have it for a gift, many would postpone getting it indefinitely, thus keeping women from hearing the message God gave me—some perhaps even missing out altogether until it was too late to help their marriages!

I have to admit that towards the end of this grueling attack, my nerves were getting somewhat frayed! I was trying to work, but I had missed so much sleep, it was difficult. My brain was going in too many directions, too. Finally I just stopped and moved to my piano and began to worship the Lord. A peace came over me and I experienced His anointing to complete my task! He is faithful to hear us when we call!

When you are reflecting on hurtful times, past or present, know that *God* didn't want to hurt you. When we sin, we leave ourselves exposed to attack. When we are ignorant of the battle waging around us, we don't put on our armor or use our weapons. When those around us are not walking in the truth, their wills can be imposed on us, especially if we are out from under the protection God longs to give us. But that can all change for good as we learn the truth! The Word tells us that His people perish for a lack of the truth, but we also flourish when we are walking in the Light of His Word!

When the Lord led the children of Israel out of Egypt, He didn't lead them on the road through the Philistine country, even though it was shorter. He knew that if they faced fighting a war, they might change their minds and go back to Egypt! He is so wise in His dealings with us! If any of us knew what the road ahead would bring, we might also prefer to just stay where we are! How lazy we are! We'd rather stay in bondage than fight to be free! But the Lord is faithful and gives us a little at a time so we can taste how sweet victory is! He doesn't give us more than we can handle. When we begin to realize how precious freedom is, we find that the effort of fighting is worth it!

There is one more list of things we can put on besides our armor, and it is found in Colossians 3:12-14.

> *Therefore, as God's chosen people, holy and dearly loved, clothe yourselves with compassion, kindness, humility, gentleness, and patience. Bear with each other and forgive whatever grievances you may have against one another. Forgive as the Lord forgave you. And over all these virtues put on love, which binds them all together in perfect unity.*

Verse 15 tells us that we have been called to peace, and that is true as far as how we relate to other people! They are not the enemy! We can actually decide to put on love and the other virtues mentioned above. One thing is for sure—we need to fight the devil, that ancient dragon, but we need to live at peace with our spouses!

Does God approve of stealing? (Hint: No! See the Ten Commandments! If you can no longer find a copy at the local courthouse, look them up in Exodus 20!) Then He doesn't approve of Satan stealing your peace, joy, faith, finances, or marriage, either!

We all talk about the attack on marriage and the family in the United States today, but why aren't we fighting back?

Look again at the weapons we can use! This is WAR! Don't just lie back and take it!

8. Granting a Royal Pardon

Volumes have been written about forgiveness, yet it is so crucial to our spiritual, physical, mental, emotional, and relational health that I felt this story would not be complete without a section about it. Being able to forgive can save a marriage, whereas holding onto an offense can destroy the relationship.

First, I'd like to look at the definition of forgiveness. The 1991 edition of the *New World Dictionary* defines it as 1) "to give up the wish to punish or get even with; not have hard feelings at or toward; pardon; excuse" and 2) "to give up all claim to; not demand payment for."

Over the past ten years, much research has been devoted to the effects of forgiveness on health. I found over 50,000 web sites on the topic, and the general consensus is that unforgiveness causes potentially serious health risks. Here is a partial list of the ailments that seem to be either brought on by or worsened by unforgiveness: damaged arteries, irregular heartbeat/arrhythmia, less resistance to illness or suppressed immune system, high blood pressure, high heart rate, increased muscle tension, abdominal pain, headaches including migraine, more colds and flu, impaired circulation, irritable bowel syndrome, fatigue, anxiety and stress, premenstrual tension, fibromyalgia, asthma, and sleep disorders. As for mental and emotional health, unforgiveness appears to cause more paranoia, guilt, self-loathing (both for those who were struggling with forgiving someone else and those who were having trouble forgiving themselves), distancing themselves from others, and an unwillingness to care for themselves, thus less exercise, dieting, and so on that end up affecting general physical health, too. Hope appears to be blocked, so the will to change is gone.

The May 2000 issue of *Circulation* cites a study conducted at the University of North Carolina at Chapel Hill, which states that angry people are almost three times as likely to have a heart attack or sudden cardiac death than those who are not angry. Naturally, not everybody with these diseases got them from unforgiveness, but there is enough research to document it certainly can be a contributing factor.

On the other hand, research shows a marked improvement in health in individuals studied who have been able to release or forgive those who have offended them. Benefits include improved ease of mind, reduced blood pressure, less depression, a stronger resistance to infection, and so on. There has long been evidence that prayer, faith, and church attendance lead to well-being, health or healing, and less stress, perhaps because forgiveness is taught and encouraged in those settings.

Dr. Dean Ornish is quoted on the HealthySelf web site as saying, "One of the most powerful causes of illness is what I call emotional and spiritual heart disease . . . I don't know of anything in medicine, including drugs, surgery, and diet, that has a greater impact on death and disease than the healing power of love and intimacy." Of course, that deals with more than just forgiveness, but so many potentially loving, intimate relationships are cut short due to a lack of forgiveness.

All this research merely reinforces what has been shown to be true in Scripture for centuries. My search on Scriptural references to forgiveness led me to over 100 teachings on forgiveness, not including those that deal with the topic without actually using that word! Old and New Testaments alike were full of teachings on the subject.

When Jesus taught His disciples to pray with what we usually call "The Lord's Prayer," He notably included the need to ask God for forgiveness. Interestingly enough, He paralleled God's forgiveness of us with our own ability and willingness to forgive others. Matthew 6:12 says, "Forgive us our debts, as we also have forgiven our debtors." In verses 14 and 15 we read, "For if you forgive men when they sin against you, your heavenly Father will also forgive you. But if you do not forgive men their sins, your Father will not forgive your sins."

We do not like to think God's forgiveness is conditional on anything except our accepting what Jesus did for us in shedding His blood! But we can't ignore those "if's." In fact, the concept that our forgiveness is given directly in relation to how we forgive others is repeated throughout Scripture. In Luke 6:37, Jesus says, "Do not judge, and you will not be judged. Do not condemn, and you will not be condemned. Forgive, and you will be forgiven. A good measure, pressed down, shaken together and running over, will be poured into your lap. For with the measure you use, it will be measured to you."

Look at this verse found in John 20:23. Jesus appeared to his disciples after His resurrection, filling them with great joy. What words were uppermost on His mind to leave with them before He returned to the Father in heaven? "If you forgive anyone his sins, they are forgiven; if you do not forgive them, they are not forgiven." This came right after He breathed on them and told them to receive the Holy Spirit. He knew we would need special power from on high to be able to forgive!

Forgiveness is really supposed to become a lifestyle for Christians. Jesus told his disciples that they were supposed to forgive not only seven times a day, but also seventy times seven! Math has never been my strong point, but when you do the multiplication there, you find that it's 490 times a day! If you're awake for an average of sixteen hours each day, that comes out to being awake for 960 minutes. You would need to be forgiving others *more than* every two minutes! That boils down to just refusing to take up an offense in the first place! Before you could even get upset about it, it would be time to forgive again! (See Matthew 18:21)

We read in Hebrews 9:22 that without the shedding of blood, there is no remission of sins—no forgiveness. The Old Testament law was based upon blood sacrifices and cleansing with blood. Nearly everything had to be cleansed with blood! Even in the Garden of Eden, after Adam and Eve sinned, they tried to cover themselves and their shame with fig leaves, but the Lord slew animals to cover his children with the skin. Blood had to be shed to cover their sins; He was giving us a hint or foreshadowing of what was to come in the shedding of Jesus' precious, sinless blood. The entire book of Hebrews gives a clear picture of what Jesus did by shedding His blood for us at Calvary.

The tempting thing for us to do is to require the *offender* to bleed for what he did! We want him to grovel, beg, writhe, serve, etc.! We want him to PAY! Now perhaps not everyone can identify with that concept. If you have the motivational gift of mercy, forgiveness comes easier for you than for someone who has the motivational gift of prophet, for example! The prophet sees everything as black and white—and he can list the offense, why it is so wrong, how it has affected him, and what the long-reaching effects will be on everyone! The mercy person, on the other hand, wants to consider why the person behaves in the manner he behaves and gives grace before it is even asked for.

Besides spiritual gifting, our upbringing has a huge impact on us, too, when it comes to forgiveness. My dad used to beg my mother and us children to forgive him when he'd gone on a drinking spree and missed our important activities. The next day he would feel terrific guilt, and he would grovel in the manner I mentioned above. It was because he knew he was asking us to forgive him for something that he wasn't going to quit. He would promise it wouldn't happen again, but he knew that wasn't an honest pledge. He had to beg and weep and swear to do differently in the future, because the apologies lost their effect when they had to be repeated so often. He had to be dramatic in order to convince us that THIS time would be different. That affected how I view apologies and forgiveness; unless a person repeatedly tells me how sorry he is and shows great emotion, I don't believe he means what he's saying. It also affects how I apologize to others, feeling they won't believe me and that I'll have to somehow prove to them that I mean what I'm saying. I carry tremendous guilt unless I have groveled adequately!

My father's parents were HUGE grudge-holders, too. I can still remember my Grandma Yates telling me about a disagreement she'd had with Grandpa *many* years previously—and she proudly announced that she *still* hadn't forgiven him! Hearing that story repeated many times over as a child and young person affected my concept of forgiveness! But forgiveness is, nonetheless, part of being obedient to the Lord, and it's for our own good in every way.

It's interesting that Jesus used a parable involving money when he taught about forgiveness. In Matthew 18:23-35, he tells about a king who wanted to settle accounts with his servants. There was a man who owed the king ten thousand talents, which was a measure of money comparable to millions of dollars, but the man wasn't able to pay. The master ordered that the man, his wife and children, and all he owned be sold in order to repay the debt.

Well, the servant fell to his knees and begged for mercy! He promised to pay the entire debt back eventually, and instead of giving the man time to do so, the king cancelled the debt.

Did the servant live a thankful life and show mercy to others? No! He went out and found one of his fellow servants who owed him a hundred denarii, which was comparable to just a few dollars. He grabbed this fellow servant and even began choking him! He demanded payment, and when the servant begged for mercy and promised to repay the debt, this man refused and had the debtor thrown into prison!

His fellow servants saw what had happened and reported it to the king. The king called the man in and had him imprisoned and tortured since he hadn't shown the same mercy that had been given to him.

Verse 35 is the clincher: "This is how my heavenly Father will treat each of you unless you forgive your brother from your heart." Forgiveness is simply releasing another person from owing us anything! It doesn't mean that what he did was okay. It doesn't mean it wasn't wrong. It doesn't even mean we have to go back and be best friends with the offender—we don't have to keep going back for more of the same treatment. It just means we aren't going to expect that person to repay us in any way. We are canceling any debt the person owes us over the wrong we have suffered. It's settling the accounts, NOT because the person deserves to be forgiven, but because WE have been forgiven so freely.

If we don't forgive, we are the ones who suffer for it. We end up bound to the person who offended us, and actually, we end up bound to the offense. We can't seem to escape having the same kind of thing happen to us over and over—it's as though we draw that kind of offender to us when we don't let go of it. Sometimes, if we keep hanging on and identifying with the offense, *we* even end up doing the same thing to others that was done to *us*.

God doesn't want us to just go through the motions, either. Forgiveness has to come from our hearts. It doesn't mean that we won't remember the offense, because these minds of ours are amazing computers, capable of storing lots of data! But when we realize that we are *also* guilty of breaking God's laws, then we know we have no right to stand in judgment of someone else who has done so.

The beautiful thing about this teaching is that if the Lord expects *us* to forgive to this extent, *He* will do so even *more*! He even asked that those who crucified Him be forgiven! And when we realize how much He has truly forgiven us for—how wretched we are in light of His holiness—then we love Him enough to be forgiving towards others.

There is a time for pointing out an offense to a person who has wronged us. Matthew 18:15-19 says that if someone sins against us, we are to go and show the person his fault. If he won't listen, we are to take one or two other people along with us as a witness. If he still won't listen, we are to take it to the church, and if that doesn't even work, he is to be treated like a tax collector or pagan; in Bible times, that meant that you wouldn't associate with him any longer. An unrepentant person is one who is proud. We are to forgive him, but sometimes we have to try to determine whether or not to have an ongoing relationship with the person or not. Also, sometimes in order to protect others from future harm, we have to let the offender realize what he's done and give him a chance to repent. If we break fellowship with someone like that, sometimes it's the very thing that gives God a chance to work in his life!

What if that offender was our spouse? Is there a time for breaking fellowship with our husbands? Yes, if the offense is so great that someone is being harmed. The same procedures would apply. It doesn't necessarily mean that we have to divorce our husbands, but it might mean a time of separation to see if they will repent. (This subject will be covered more completely in the chapter titled "A Kingdom Divided.")

It can be extremely difficult to forgive someone who has abused you in some way, but remember that the Lord will repay. Vengeance truly does belong to Him! (Duet. 32:35) Remember Abigail, King David's wife? When she met David, she was married to Nabal—a mean, rough, hateful man with a terrible reputation! He was a truly despicable man! He refused to feed David and his men, so they were going to kill him!

Abigail hurried to find enough food to feed the men: two hundred loaves, two bottles of wine, five sheep dressed, five measures of parched corn, a hundred clusters of raisins, and two hundred cakes of figs! She fell on her face before David and asked him to put her husband's iniquity on her; she asked him to please refrain from shedding blood and to accept the blessing she had prepared for the men. She didn't want David to lower himself to the same level as Nabal by taking matters of revenge into his own hands. David accepted her offering and changed his mind about killing Nabal. Abigail helped him avoid bringing judgment on himself. When Abigail told her husband what had happened, he had what sounds like a heart attack or stroke and died ten days later. And Abigail ended up being married to David!

In this case, Abigail had a husband who definitely was not doing what was right! But it was not her job to correct him. She honored his position as her husband, and the Lord dealt with Nabal. He did so without anyone else having to take matters into his own hands.

Bitterness progresses if left undealt with. I can't remember who taught on the subject, but somewhere I learned that it starts with holding a grudge for wrong suffered. Then comes wrath, which is getting hot to the boiling point. Next is anger, releasing pent up feeling. Following the anger is clamoring, which is to yell. Slander is the next step, and it is to defame or belittle someone and to take away from that person in some way. Malice is the final step, which involves doing bodily harm.

The Lord wants us to be kind, compassionate, and forgiving! According to Ephesians 4:32, we can get rid of bitterness: "Be kind and compassionate to one another, forgiving each other, just as in Christ God forgave you." He wants to help us let go. Get to the root of it—find out where it's coming from. It does not always come from a huge offense; sometimes it stems from a small wrong that was allowed to go untreated. Realize that if you don't deal with it, it *will* grow! In fact, it can take over, like a bind weed that takes over the entire flower bed!

One member of our family, a daughter, has caused great pain to the rest of us. I believe all of the rest of us have had to deal with bitterness towards this person. I certainly have had to face it. I resented her. I resented how hard she made my life. I resented some sin she brought into our family. I resented the extra time and attention she demanded. I let a root of bitterness take hold.

When we were considering the name for our last baby, we went back to one we'd had picked out since expecting our second child: Anna Marie. Anna means "full of grace," and Marie means "bitterness." When Anna was born, I knew that the Lord was letting me know that there is grace for my bitterness. It was one more reminder that I needed to let go of it—and that I could do so with God's grace.

With time and much prayer, along with falling short many times along the way, I have been able to work past the pain in my relationship with this daughter. I know she is hurting, and "hurt people hurt people." She was estranged from our family for about five years, but she is gradually becoming a part of us again. In fact, she recently introduced me to her current boyfriend as her adoptive mother, which was a great improvement from telling people I was just the woman she used to live with! Other members of our family are at various stages in their attempts to let go of bitterness and unforgiveness towards her. Sadly, some are making no attempt whatsoever.

Bitterness is an ugly thing. Do you know a woman who is just *sweet*? That is a woman who does not have a root of bitterness! What kinds of things steal the sweetness from a woman? Sin; being hurt deeply or repeatedly without working through the forgiveness issues; being unloved—or thinking you are unloved, which is not the same thing; putting self first; others' examples ("Bad company corrupts good morals."); taking up someone else's offense; being around lots of hurting people, such as having a job with domestic violence or rape victims or abused children or prisoners, where you see a side of society that is perverted and wicked day after day.

Try a little exercise here if you think you have lost some of your sweetness through the years. Write down the thing or things that you think might have taken it away. Then begin to give each of those situations to the Lord. Is there someone you need to forgive? Then forgive and release them whether or not they deserve it. Go to the Maker, and ask Him to restore you and make you whole. Ask Him to help you be gracious; there's nothing as ugly as a mean, hard, old woman! Except possibly a mean, hard old man!

Be content where you are. Who is responsible for your present condition? Not God! He does want to help, though. Blaming others and wasting time in wishful thinking only delay your healing. Living with vain regrets for the past pulls you down, too. The Lord wants to make us sweet again, but we have to let go of the bitterness so He can do something eternal.

Realizing that we aren't really fighting against flesh and blood can help us forgive and release people. Our real enemies are Satan and his cohorts! (Ephesians 6)

My Aunt Audrey says that if we're carrying an offense against someone, we've dropped either our sword (the Word of God) or our shield (faith), because you only have two hands to carry with!

Our spouses probably hurt, offend, and wrong us more than anyone else, partially because they live with us, so the opportunity presents itself more often, and also because we expect so much from them. But we need to release them and give them the same kind of grace the Lord has given us, AND the same kind we want them to extend to us when we wrong them. Ephesians 4:32 says, "Be kind and compassionate to one another, forgiving each other, just as in Christ God forgave you." Forgive. Your health—in every sense of the word—depends on it!

9. A Kingdom Divided

Jesus said that a kingdom divided against itself will be ruined and a house divided against itself will fall (Luke 11:17). He was replying to people who were accusing him of driving out demons by the power of Satan, but it is a truth that applies to anything that is supposed to be united. How true that in marriage, if we can't or won't find some common ground, the relationship doesn't stand.

Chances are, more than half of you reading this book have been divorced. Your feelings about that could vary widely, ranging from guilt to defeat to anger to relief—and who knows how many other emotions I haven't even mentioned! In most cases, large doses of pain and disappointment have been part of the process, too. Probably most of the rest of you who haven't ever been divorced (myself included!) have been sorely tempted to join the ranks of those who have ended their marriages! I want to offer hope to all of you, regardless of what your experience has been.

Statistics say that now there is a higher percentage of divorce in the church than outside it. I've wondered why that is, and think that perhaps it is partially due to the fact that Christians more often decide to get married than people outside the church, because they know that God's Word says unmarried sex is sin. So if a higher percent are marrying, then it stands to reason that a higher percent of them could have unhappy marriages since they have more marriages overall. Just a theory!

It could also be because we have been programmed to believe that as God's children, we deserve a special form of happiness that the world doesn't have. (After all, since God loves us, wouldn't He want us happy?) We don't understand what it takes to find happiness in marriage or life, and when our union turns out to be a disappointment in that regard, we want out.

After teaching junior high students for several years, I believe that "going out" at such a young age also contributes to the way we view commitment. These kids are pledging to "love" just this *one* person—but only until their feelings are hurt or someone "better" comes along. It's practice for divorce!

Christians also sometimes have some odd ideas about whom they are "meant" to marry. Some married people begin to think they've married the "wrong" person, and when their lust overtakes them in a desired relationship with someone outside of marriage, they convince themselves that the Lord has finally brought them their soul mates, and He is smiling in approval at the newly found love, blessing the trip down the road to divorce court so they can be free to marry again. Not only is that *not true* according to what God's Word says about divorce, but it's also just plain *hogwash*!

Of course, divorce is rampant throughout our society, not just in the church. I believe that the whole procedure usually used for finding a mate in America today contributes to our high divorce rate. We need to realize that dating and marrying someone we have "fallen in love" with is a relatively new concept in the world. Only in the past 100 years or so has it been practiced, and with disastrous results. In days past, when parents arranged marriages, couples went into the relationship with far different expectations, and their divorce rate was much lower than their modern and post-modern counterparts. Perhaps it's time to take the best from both worlds, marrying someone we find appealing, yet with discretion and advice from our parents and trusted counselors, all the time expecting that the initial feelings will come and go, but real love will grow if we are willing to learn and change from a self-centered focus to one of meeting the needs of another person!

In fact, there is a couple that was featured on the Early Show on CBS on October 10, 2003. This couple embarked upon an experiment to see if they would be able to fall in love with the help of counselors. They did! They had been strangers before; now their biggest problem is that they live far apart and haven't figured out yet how to be together!

Most of us wouldn't want to go so far as to marry a stranger or have someone else arrange our marriages! So what qualities should a person look for when seeking a spouse if we're trying to lay a foundation for a marriage that will stand the test of time? Most of us spend far more time planning the *wedding* than planning the *marriage*! This is so sad, considering the statistics. Only 25% of all first marriages in the U.S. endure and are happy. Twenty percent of them fail within the first five years, 33% fail with in ten years, and 43% fail within fifteen years. Perhaps we need to take more time to plan a successful union!

The Bible is the guidebook for Christians. What does it tell us about finding a spouse? The clearest direction is found in I Corinthians 6:14-17; it says that we should not be unequally yoked with unbelievers. Although there are other things to look for, that has to remain the number one factor. Is the person a believer in Jesus Christ? Not just someone who once repeated a prayer, but rather someone who is committed to the Lord and truly wants to follow Him all his life. DO NOT DATE SOMEONE WHO DOES NOT PROFESS JESUS CHRIST AS LORD AND SAVIOR! You end up falling in love with people you spend time with, so don't spend time with someone who is not a good candidate for marriage according to the guidelines of the Bible! And don't make the common mistake of thinking you can change your spouse once you've said the "I do's"!

Even if someone is a believer, see if there is a fit with theology and how the other person approaches Christianity. If one of you is a Charismatic who speaks in tongues, enjoys singing choruses beamed on the wall via overhead projector, and clapping and dancing before the Lord during worship, while the other is a reserved Episcopalian who prefers a liturgical service with majestic organ music filling the cathedral with traditional hymns of the faith, corporate reading of the Scriptures, and silent, private prayers, then you might run into disunity!

Then see how you agree or differ on practical matters. For instance, do you both want to have children? Do you share any of the same interests? Can you laugh together? Do you like to be around other people or stay home alone? Have you received a similar amount of education?

On a more serious note, make sure you ask those who are close to you if they see any red flags about your intended. Are there anger issues? Control issues? Dominance issues? Do your family and friends find your potential mate moody? Rude? Lazy? Don't be afraid to find out how they perceive the character of this person. When you are "in love," you really can't see as clearly as those who love you, those who aren't being blinded by emotion. Of course, no one is perfect, but you do need to pay attention to major character flaws.

Even looking at the person's family background is important. Is there a history of unfaithfulness? Child abuse? Sexual abuse? Divorce? Alcoholism? You won't necessarily have to rule out a mate based on the family background, but realize that the sins of the father are passed down to the third and fourth generations, so you will need to be aware of what you are up against (Exodus 20:5). So often, those sins show up again in the children, grandchildren, and great grandchildren. Know what you're getting into. You also need to determine whether or not you can get along with the family of your potential spouse. Is the family open and welcoming to you, or do you sense resistance? Better find out why, if you do!

Even birth order affects relationships! I'm the oldest of six and Tracy is the youngest of two! We come from different worlds with different expectations of life and love! It made me naturally bossy and he was obviously pampered as the baby!

Are you really compatible? Intensely appealing chemistry can be mistaken for compatibility, but it is usually based on sexual attractiveness and drive. It can also be a false attraction stemming from our childhoods and what feels "normal" to us based on how we were brought up. (Remember Robin Norwood's book *Women Who Love too Much.*)

All these factors are so important that it really makes sense to have a long engagement. It takes time to see who the person really is, as well as to reveal your own true character. You won't get to know each other if you simply put your best foot forward all the time, and in a long engagement, it becomes impossible to do that continuously. You want to be loved for who you really are, not for the image you have portrayed. That doesn't mean that you should be selfish and rude! But let your true nature come through and be honest about your expectations and desires in marriage and family. No matter how attractive another person seems, those qualities will fade quickly if you are not a good match in temperament and world view and goals.

So often, we make the decision about whom to marry while we are still so young and inexperienced we don't even know what *we* like and want out of life, much less discern those qualities in another person! Or we make the decision before we have healed from a previous relationship. That is why the main ingredient is genuine shared faith, then a shared commitment to keep the covenant before God. All the other issues and situations can be lived through, even if it ends up being a hard relationship. Once you have made the commitment and covenanted with another person in marriage, the time for checking out those qualities is over! If you feel you made a mistake, please don't rush out and potentially make another one by ending the relationship.

We are not here on earth to find happiness; we are here to know and serve God and to become more like Him! When we do that, we can find *more* happiness, even in a relationship that was NOT a good fit in the natural realm. Tracy and I had so little in common when we married! After we married, we took a compatibility test and learned that we are the LEAST compatible personality types! But since we are committed to each other, the Lord, and our family, we have been able to find areas we can enjoy together. It has been gradual, but steady.

Michael Phillips and Judith Pella have co-authored several delightful novels, and I found the concepts about married love in *Shadows over Stonewycke* to be on target! One of the characters, Logan, has a lot to learn—here is what he was told:

> *"What has falling in love to do with marriage? Nothing! I hope that someday soon you leave behind this foolishness about being 'in love.' No marriage can survive unless it gets past that and to the love of sacrifice. Ah, but you are young!" [Logan replies, "But you said your wife loved you. I assume you love her?"] "Of course! Of course! We are in love now because we first learned how to sacrifice ourselves one to the other. We have learned to serve, to lay down our lives, to wash each other's feet, so to speak. You don't do those kinds of things year after year unless you are determined to love. Not in love, but determined to love . . . . Love—that comes second! First comes commitment, sacrifice. Then, and only then, comes true and lasting love. That is why my wife and I are now in love." (p. 170)*

Later in the book, Logan's wife Allison is beginning to realize that she has much to learn about what love really is, too. She is reflecting with her brother:

> *"Love has so many aspects . . . almost none of which a young couple getting married is aware of. I'm learning so many ways in which it's different than what I always thought it to be. You always think love is an emotion you feel toward another. And to now come to realize it's not that at all but rather how you behave toward others—it's quite an awakening, to say the least. And to think that in our eight years together, I never really loved Logan in a true sense, never really put him before myself, despite all the so-called love I felt for him." (p. 241)*

So perhaps our expectations have not prepared us for what marriage will really be. Unfortunately, we find many other stresses leading to disappointment and unmet needs that make us *want* to be free from our covenant.

Jealousy can rear its ugly head and cause problems. You might remember my sharing that when I was in high school, I was convinced my mother should leave my father because he gave her the third degree every time she came home from the grocery store or beauty salon. What took her so long?

Whom did she see? Who talked to her? And on and on the questions went. I thought Mama should just leave him and get a life! Of course, my attitude was of the world, not God's Word, so I'm thankful she didn't listen to me!

Insecure people are often jealous, and proud people can also struggle with that green-eyed monster! Read this account of King David's wife and the consequences she had to deal with for her attitude.

> *When David returned home to bless his household, Michal daughter of Saul came out to meet him and said, "How the king of Israel has distinguished himself today, disrobing in the sight of the slave girls of his servants as any vulgar fellow would!"*
>
> *David said to Michal, "It was before the Lord, who chose me rather than your father or anyone from his house when he appointed me ruler over the Lord's people Israel—I will celebrate before the Lord. I will become even more undignified than this, and I will be humiliated in my own eyes. But by these slave girls you spoke of, I will be held in honor."*
>
> *And Michal daughter of Saul had no children to the day of her death. (2 Samuel 6:20-23)*

David was coming home to bless his household, but Michal jumped the gun and started griping him out before he even got inside the palace! She disdained him, not because what he was doing was actually wrong, but because she was totally eaten up with jealousy. She couldn't stand it that he was "undressed" in front of the servant girls! She was insecure!

They had a disagreement, and Michal missed out on whatever blessing David was bringing to her and their household. I wonder how many times I've also missed a blessing because of the way I've interacted with Tracy!

Think about her attacking him before he even got in the door, too! When our husbands get home, do we even consider that they might be tired or have a lot on their minds? Or can we hardly wait for them to show up so we can start in with our questions, complaints, and needs? What would happen if we waited for them to come in, relax, eat some dinner, and catch their breath before we bombarded them? What benefits would we receive by simply thinking of what they need instead of only our own agendas?

For many years, I thought the Lord caused Michal to be childless as punishment for her actions and words and attitudes that day—and that might be what happened. But it might be that David just didn't go to bed with her anymore! He had other wives who weren't giving him that kind of grief!

Another character flaw that can cause a rift in a marriage is when one or both have a critical spirit. That is something in my heritage that I am not proud of, and it affected the way I viewed my spouse for many years. My paternal grandparents received great joy from criticizing others. For entertainment, they would park on Main Street in Hutchinson, Kansas, and make fun of people who passed by! It's true—that was what they did for fun! They would go to the Kansas State Fair, simply for the enjoyment of sitting in the park there to watch the myriad of people who would walk by! Believe me, the Kansas State Fair provided ample selection to whet their appetites for the outlandish and strange!

Sometimes they would take us grandchildren along for the ride. I can still remember watching one elderly gentleman walk past us on the sidewalk in downtown Hutchinson. Now, looking back, I realize that he was probably an alcoholic or mentally ill, but as a youngster, I didn't have that kind of insight. He paused often, took a hankie out of his pocket, and polished the parking meters or light poles. He was dirty and unshaven. My grandparents laughed till they almost cried. How sad to be teaching small children to poke fun at an individual who was obviously hurting and needy! Still, that was how it was with my grandparents, in spite of great qualities they possessed in other areas.

My mother brought an entirely different set of values to the table! She was kind-hearted, and if she had known where Grandma and Grandpa were taking us, that would have been the end of the outings! She had a positive impact on my father's family, bringing much more civilization to them than they'd known before she became part of the family!

My father, though, grew up with great criticism, and he carried it on into our family at home. I can remember being criticized for how I ate—he told me I looked like a duck; then he demonstrated my swooping down to my plate to get a bite. How it hurt! I wanted his approval desperately but he didn't know how to give it until long after I had left home.

Guess how I turned out? Critical of others! Insecurity breeds criticism, and I must have had large doses of it, if the way I criticized others was any indication! I made fun of how people looked, how they talked, their performances, their beliefs, their attitudes, actions, personalities, and beyond! It is SO embarrassing to admit it now, but I even went through our school and church directories to make a determination as to whether or not someone was pretty or ugly! I pronounced judgment on others for everything I could think of!

Unfortunately, that trait was foremost in my marriage, as well. Tracy had already lost before he ever began! He couldn't do anything "right" in my eyes! I cut him down so many times, I don't even know how the man was able to keep going! If *he* had talked to *me* that way or shown the disapproval to me that *I* showed to *him*, I wouldn't have been able to stand it!

It took me years to realize that I had no right to be critical of him! I'm not God! I have no idea how past experiences have influenced who Tracy is today, and I need to realize what God's grace is working into him! The Lord is in charge and is well able to change all of us! Criticism is NOT co-existent with love! What arrogance to think I have the knowledge, time, or right to sit in judgment of someone else! When I see clearly, I realize that I have a full-time job just trying to get my *own* life in order!

We are measured with whatever measuring stick we use on others, according to the Word. I want to be loved and accepted in spite of my own shortcomings, so I must extend the same grace to others! Criticism is just another form of pride showing up—I must think I'm better, or I wouldn't assume I have the right to point the finger! Lord, forgive me and change me!

My mouth gets me in more trouble than anything else! Really, it's the heart issues that remain unresolved, because out of the abundance of the heart, the mouth speaks! Here's what Proverbs 30:32 has to say about that: "If you have played the fool and exalted yourself, or if you have planned evil, clap your hand over your mouth!" How true! We need to recognize our errors quickly and try to take them back! We can't, of course, but we can immediately stop when we realize it and try to make it right. Pride sure gets us in trouble!

Guilt is another pitfall in marriages because it affects relationships so deeply, our own guilt as well as the other person's guilt. Unconfessed sin zaps our strength. Psalm 32:3-5 reads, "When I kept silent, my bones wasted away through my groaning all day long. For day and night Your hand was heavy upon me; my strength was sapped as in the heat of summer. Then I acknowledged my sin to you and did not cover up my iniquity. I said, 'I will confess my transgressions to the Lord'—and You forgave the guilt of my sin." Wow! What freedom comes when we pour it out on the throne of grace! It lifts a load that we sometimes don't even realize we've been carrying!

When we have sinned, we want to hide. We know the sin is obvious; our eyes reveal it, because they are the windows to our souls. We avoid eye contact because we are ashamed. Everyone sins, but we can begin to get victory over sin if we willingly let the light of God's Word shine on those areas. Darkness flees in the presence of Light! Then we have nothing left to hide!

A day will come when everything will come to light, and our motives will be exposed. (I Corinthians 4:5) I'd much rather bring my heart to the light NOW while I can repent and be forgiven and grow than having it forced open and exposed when there is no chance for having it cleaned up!

If we are willing to admit when we're wrong, we can see tremendous growth. 1 John 1:9 says, "If we confess our sins, He is faithful and just and will forgive us our sins and cleanse us from all unrighteousness." Sometimes when we have struggled with a particular sin for a long time, crying over it, asking for forgiveness, yet finding ourselves trapped by it, the key to breaking free can be confession. Finding a trusted confidante can make us accountable and be the very thing that gives us victory. Hopefully we already believe the Lord forgives us; it's the cleansing from unrighteousness that sometimes eludes us! Accountability is a step towards walking in the light where sin cannot dwell! Proverbs 28:13 "He who conceals his sins does not prosper, but whoever confesses and renounces them finds mercy."

Realize that there is a place for guilt: it is to show us our need for repentance. When we have sinned, we ARE guilty! But that doesn't mean we have to grovel or wallow in it. We can be forgiven. In Luke 18, we read about a Pharisee and a tax collector. The Pharisee was proud and thanked God that he was not like other men he considered sinners. He gave a list of his good credentials that he felt should earn him favor with God. But the tax collector wouldn't even look up to heaven. Instead, he beat his breast upon the realization of his unworthiness and guilt, asking God to have mercy on him since he was a sinner! He was sorry and knew how dark and ugly his humanity was! And Jesus said that this sinner was the one who was justified before God! Let your real guilt lead you to humble repentance before God.

See how the heavenly Father felt about Ephraim when he sinned (Jeremiah 31:20). " 'Is not Ephraim my dear son, the child in whom I delight? Though I often speak against him, I still remember him. Therefore my heart yearns for him; I have great compassion for him,' declares the Lord." Realize that the

Lord loves you, even when He has had to discipline you or correct you or let you suffer your own consequences for poor choices. He remembers you. His heart yearns for you. He has compassion on you. You are His child in whom He delights if you have asked Him into your life. He will hear you when you respond to His discipline. He wants to give you a new beginning with Him!

If you've asked God to forgive you, but you are still feeling terribly guilty, the devil is probably working on your conscience. The Bible tells us in Hebrews 10:22 that even our conscience can be sprinkled clean. That's where faith comes in—faith that what Jesus did for us at Calvary was good enough. Sometimes we get pride, only in reverse, thinking our sin is SO big that even Jesus' blood can't cover it! Not true! His sacrifice for our sin was perfect, and God the Father accepted it as payment. So if you have truly repented and confessed, don't accept those bad feelings about it anymore. Tell the devil to shut his mouth and leave you alone! Say out loud that you are forgiven! Write the Scripture on index cards and leave them where you can see them regularly until you begin to believe it! This will go a long way toward marital health if you are no longer carrying around the burden of your own sin!

Another area that is closely related to guilt is carrying secrets. If you are one with your spouse, then your hand is his hand. Now, the Scripture says that you should not let your left hand know what your right hand is doing, but that does NOT refer to keeping secrets in marriage! I know that some of you feel there are things you simply can't tell your spouse, and you might be right. You know him better than anyone else, so you probably have a good idea of what pushes his buttons!

But do you realize that the fear of being found out is affecting your relationship? Secrets come between you tangibly because you are not confident of your husband's love. The enemy of your soul can torment you subconsciously by saying that if your husband knew everything about you, your character, and your actions, then he wouldn't love you. Sometimes you need to call the devil's bluff! So often, you carry a weight that your husband could have and would have gladly helped you bear if you had just brought him into the situation. Even if he is angry at first—and probably more so if you've kept the secret for a long time—it might be exactly what is needed to bring the two of you closer. Carefully weigh out the secret compared to the freedom that would come from honesty. Seek godly counsel about whether or not to share your secret with your husband. A pastor or close friend will probably be able to help you figure out what is best in your situation if you aren't sure. If you still believe you must keep the secret, do so, but make sure you are limiting the number of secrets you have to a minimum.

Job 12:2, speaking of God, says, "His eyes are on the ways of men; He sees their every step. There is no dark place, no deep shadow, where evildoers can hide." Be assured that there is nothing hidden from Him. He knows you best and still loves you most!

Sometimes issues from our past can hold us back from a happy marriage. I'm reminded of a line from the movie "Runaway Bride," where Julia Robert's character Maggie says, "I think there is a distinct possibility that I am profoundly and irreversibly screwed up." Can anyone identify with that revelation? Some things are hidden deeply in us. Therapists and counselors want to dig deeply to find the keys from the past that are affecting the present, and there can be an element of benefit from doing so. But the Lord is the One Who sees it all. He knows what lies in darkness and all that has gone before. Uncovering it isn't enough; we also need healing for those dark things. Often release and forgiveness are keys to healing. For sure, continuing in a relationship with Jesus Christ and fellowshipping with a group of accepting, loving group of godly believers will help you make huge strides towards wholeness. This is another area where progress is not always overnight, but building trusting relationships over time will make a real difference.

Some of us also thwart our potential for marital happiness and unity because we are still searching for our daddy's love and approval. We look for love but remain unsatisfied. It is so important for fathers to really love their daughters! Dads can help their daughters feel cherished, beautiful, talented, smart, and loved. When dads complete their girls in this way, they are also setting a high standard for the type of treatment the girls will expect from men; it will go a long ways towards protecting them from accepting any bullying behavior from men!

Mothers, if your husband is not giving that to your daughters, don't think that you need to bail out of the marriage and find someone who will give that to your daughters. It doesn't work that way! She will still be looking for her own daddy's love. Instead, be an example to your daughter of what it means to let Jesus meet your needs first! Show her how to love unconditionally! Respect your husband in front of her, and teach her to honor him. That will do more for their relationship than you can imagine! And as your husband has his needs for respect met, he will be freer to give of himself. If we can let Jesus heal us where we missed out on that kind of father's love, then we can pattern an example for our daughters that will benefit them throughout their lives.

Frankly, having women in the work force has also contributed greatly to the demise of marriage and family. There are far more temptations in the office or on business trips than there are at home. At work, men and women are generally at their best. They are showered, dressed nicely, hair and grooming taken care of, etc. They are also away from the stresses of running a household or rearing children. They are there to do a job, and they are focused. Someone of the opposite sex who is spending time with them, talking to them, helping them with projects, expressing concern for their well-being, and so on, can really capture their attention! Some people spend far more time sharing with others at work than they do at home with their spouses. And the sharing is often not the stressful kind.

So if a woman is working, she will need to keep her guard up to a certain degree. She will need to be careful not to send a signal that she is available or interested in a relationship with a male co-worker, and she will need to watch out for signals from men at work who might be interested in her. There is no such thing as "harmless" flirting! Be professional if you choose to work! Spend lots of time in prayer for protection from the enemy's devices!

God knew in advance that we would be tempted. But when we take our wedding vows, we promise that if and when temptation presents itself, we will FORSAKE all others! That means we won't leave our husbands alone or abandon them.

Whoever wrote the wedding vows KNEW sometimes it would be "worse" instead of "better"! Most of us realized going into marriage that it wouldn't always be perfect, but somehow we didn't realize it would really be THAT much worse! Our generation doesn't think we deserve to go through any of the worse stages. But it's HARD to live with another person! If you don't think it is hard, then perhaps you've had a nice, normal upbringing that prepared you for life, but MOST of us haven't! And sad to say, we aren't giving that kind of upbringing to our children, either, because we're still working through our own issues! Lord, help us!

Okay, so these are several factors that can contribute to our desire to end the marriage covenant. But is it okay to divorce based on these character flaws or disappointments?

There is much confusion about divorce, simply because we often look to counselors and attorneys before even going to God's Word. What does the Bible have to say about divorce? I found thirty-three references to divorce, and these passages sum up the general teachings on the subject that apply to us.

Deuteronomy 24:1 states that if a man finds his wife displeasing because he finds something indecent about her, he is allowed to give her a certificate of divorce. This is written by Moses under the Lord's direction. We don't find a list here of what is considered indecent, but later, in Matthew 19, we see the Pharisees trying to trap Jesus with this law. They ask him if Moses really commanded that a man could give his wife a certificate of divorce for any and every reason.

> *"Haven't you read," he replied, "that at the beginning the Creator made them male and female, and said, 'For this reason a man will leave his father and mother and be united to his wife, and two will become one flesh'? So they are no longer two, but one. Therefore what God has joined together, let man not separate."*
>
> *"Why then," they asked, "did Moses command that a man give his wife a certificate of divorce and send her away?"*
>
> *Jesus replied, "Moses permitted you to divorce your wives because your hearts were hard. But it was not this way from the beginning. I tell you that anyone who divorces his wife, except for marital unfaithfulness, and marries another woman commits adultery." Matt. 19:4-8*

Even when the Lord refers to His relationship with Israel, he uses the word *divorce* to describe how He has cast her away—because of her adulteries! (See Jeremiah 3) He makes it clear how He views divorce in Malachi 2:13-16:

> *Another thing you do: You flood the Lord's altar with tears. You weep and wail because He no longer pays attention to your offerings or accepts them with pleasure from your hands. You ask, "Why?" It is because the Lord is acting as the witness between you and the wife of your youth, because you have broken faith with her, though she is your partner, the wife of your marriage covenant.*
>
> *Has not the Lord made them one? In flesh and spirit they are His. And why one? Because He was seeking godly offspring. So guard yourself in your spirit, and do not break faith with the wife of your youth.*

"I hate divorce," says the Lord God of Israel, "and I hate a man's covering himself with violence as well as with his garment," says the Lord Almighty.

So guard yourself in your spirit, and do not break faith.

This shows us that divorce can even hinder our prayers and offerings from being accepted by God. He speaks of violence in the same sentence as divorce, perhaps because in divorcing, you are violently ripping apart what He has made one.

It appears that God doesn't recognize divorce except for adultery, even if the courts do. Does this mean that if adultery has occurred, a couple HAS to divorce? It doesn't appear so. Jesus says it is permitted only because of the hardness of our hearts. Other reasons for divorce aren't even acknowledged by Him. We need to remember that in the Old Testament times, adultery was punishable by stoning, too! Sometimes divorce wasn't even an option—the offender wouldn't even be around to BE divorced! Yet a man could quietly serve his wife with divorce papers rather than having her stoned.

This was what Joseph was planning to do with Mary, his betrothed, when he learned of her pregnancy. Naturally, he thought she had committed adultery—she was pregnant! He knew he hadn't had sex with her, and this was in the days before test tube babies, so adultery was the only other reason he knew of that she could have possibly been impregnated! Of course, we know that the angel told Joseph the miraculous origin of her conception, but he would have quietly divorced her if he hadn't learned the truth. (Note: Even though they were only betrothed and not actually married yet, the betrothal carried a complete commitment with it just as a marriage would. Some translations say that Joseph planned to "put her way quietly" rather than using the word divorce, but they really meant essentially the same thing.)

For years I have pondered what Jesus meant by our "hardness of heart." Maybe He was referring to the hardness of the heart of the person who committed the adultery. Perhaps He knew that in some cases, that person would be too hardhearted to change or let the Lord keep him or her faithful.

It's also possible that the hardheartedness He spoke of could occur on the part of the wounded one. The pain of the unfaithfulness could cause a wall of protection to be erected, a hardness to set in, a bitterness to consume the soul, resulting in an unwillingness to forgive. Matthew 13:15 says, "For this people's heart has become calloused; they hardly hear with their ears, and they have closed their eyes. Otherwise, they might see with their eyes, hear with their ears, understand with their hearts and turn, and I would heal them."

When I started thinking about the calloused heart, it made me really think about what makes a callous. My daddy used to get callouses on his hands when digging postholes. I remember seeing the blisters the first day, then after several days of digging, the blisters hardened, forming callouses. If he had continued to dig, he wouldn't have even felt the pain anymore because the hardened skin eventually protected him from suffering.

When I first learned to play my guitar, the pain was also intense. It hurt badly if I hadn't played for a long time, then led worship for several services at a retreat, too—ouch! We willingly endure certain kinds of pain in order to reach a desired result.

But I have no choice about the callous on the bottom of my left foot. It is caused from walking on a bone spur. I have to keep it trimmed just to *endure* walking. No matter how many times I trim it, the callous comes back; then I keep irritating it by putting pressure on that bone spur again every time I walk. Trimming it causes damage to the surrounding tissues and it becomes a vicious cycle. Only removing the bone spur, the source of the pain, would bring lasting relief.

All of us will be hurt in our hearts! It is inevitable! But how we perceive the pain and deal with it determines the outcome. We can forgive the offender and embrace the experience, knowing we'll gain something from it. There might still be evidence of the wound, but it doesn't hurt anymore. Or we can hold on to the pain, reliving it, and "trimming away" only enough of it to keep going, but never building up the resistance that allows us to move past the pain. We can't always avoid the *person* through whom the pain comes, but we *can* decide to forgive completely, thus removing the true source of pain: the wound.

Time does NOT heal all wounds! They can fester over time, getting worse! If we treat the wound correctly first, then time can do its work. But when we've been deeply wounded, and we haven't dealt with it, we are in for lengthy, painful times ahead that can bring an end to our marriages.

I know firsthand that a willingness to forgive and keep the commitment of marriage is possible in situations like this. Not that I am a quick forgiver, because I'm not! Remember, I come from a long line of grudge holders! Tracy and I faced a situation that could have turned out badly for our entire family, but God's grace helped us through it, and now, looking back, we know it was worth working through the hardness of heart we both experienced.

There was a time when I had a biblical "reason" to divorce Tracy. (You may wonder why I'm not explaining what he did. The Bible tells us to confess our *own* faults, not our brothers'! Knowing the offense won't help you in any way, so I'm not going to name it. You might decide to compare what your own husband has done and try to determine which was worse so you can gauge whether or not you should stay in the marriage or leave him! That's the LAST thing I would want you to consider when making such an important decision! So it will remain private, confessed to those Tracy needed to confess it to, but otherwise just between us unless the Lord nudges him to share it someday!) It involved something that had happened several years before I found out about it.

At the time I found out about his sin, we were foster parenting four of our kids until they were available for adoption. I felt I had an obligation to them; they had been through enough, having their birth family already ripped from them. I wasn't going to put them through the uncertainty that would come from a split in our family at that time. I knew that if I did, it would probably mean they would be placed in yet another home. So I decided to wait until the adoption was done, then if it still seemed necessary, I'd make a decision about our marriage.

My heart was solid rock. There was nothing virtuous about my decision—I didn't want to be with Tracy. At that time, I still had not really learned to love him with an unconditional, godly love, and this situation inflamed hatred towards him in my heart.

Any progress we'd made in our marriage was out of reach. We were way more than back at square one—we were in a pit! To make matters worse, Tracy started working nights, which further strained our already uncomfortable family life. Truth be known, though, it might have been a blessing in disguise, because the children hardly ever saw him; they were saved from seeing how poorly we were getting along. Still, it was a crucial time for Nathan, who was going through adolescence and all the needs of a young man to be involved with his father. I had just suffered my ninth miscarriage, too, and was just about ready to throw in the towel on facing daily life.

> *July 14, 1994 It's a little after 4 A.M. I'm back to feeling like it's just the Lord and me. I guess for a long while I've wanted to lean on someone else—hoping it*

would be Tracy, trying to consider him and let him lead as much as he could. But now I'm feeling like I need to go ahead and do what's right for my family. For instance, I'm having devotions with them. If I wait for Tracy to do it, it won't get done. They need the input now. I'm also planning some fun activities for them.

It's sad, but our evenings are peaceful with Tracy on night shift. It takes away a lot of stress since it's clear who's in charge. I am when he's gone. When he's home, he should be, but won't take the initiative, thereby leaving us all hanging and making my role unclear. I hate it! When he's home, he's so cranky, too—doesn't know how to minister to us—or just be pleasant to be around. Lord, help us. . . .

I put my life and the lives of those I love into Your hands. You are ***God*** *and* ***Lord*** *of us.*

Ps. 94:18-19 "When I said, 'My foot is slipping,' Your love, O Lord, supported me. When anxiety was great within me, Your consolation brought joy to my soul."

There really aren't words capable of describing how awful this time was for us. The distrust, anger, accusations, and pain were overwhelming. I made life miserable for Tracy, and I really don't believe many men could have lived through my demands. I told him that the only way I would stay with him was if he would agree to be totally accountable to me—I was to be free to ask him anything, not only about his actions, but even his thoughts! I put the man through torture! I was self-righteous and made myself the judge, jury, and jailer all at once! Not that he didn't deserve it—he did! Where was the Old Testament judgment when I needed it—for him, of course, never for me!

But what is grace about? What is unmerited favor? The love of God is shown in that "while we were still sinners, Christ died for us" (Romans 5:8). He gave us love and forgiveness even though we didn't deserve it, but I didn't understand how that was to be lived out in personal relationships. I had quickly forgotten the grace and unconditional love Tracy had shown me during my own indiscretions years before. I made him *pay*, throwing his sin in his face repeatedly. I rose up in indignation at the slightest hint of imperfection in his life, never seeing that I was carrying my own burdens of sin. It was the ugliest time of our lives, and there was absolutely no hope in my heart for a future of peace, much less love.

The Lord is so faithful, though, even when we are not! He patiently waited for me to get past the anger enough to hear

Him, and He gently began to show me the self-righteousness of my own heart. I really thought I was better than Tracy. It took months of the Lord working patiently with me to show me that I was no better—that my own sin was just as disgusting in His eyes as anything the worst sinner in the world was capable of. It is only His grace in our lives that keeps us from being totally depraved and corrupt! I didn't realize that I had to come to a place of humility, and it took the Lord stripping me of much of my identity up to that point before I could begin to change.

Remember when I shared that after Tracy learned of my indiscretion, he actually faced the part he had played in not meeting my needs? It did not excuse me in any way, but it was an important step for him in working through forgiveness towards me. Well, the Lord gently began to show me during this time of dealing with Tracy's error, that I also needed to look at the ways my behavior had contributed to his sin. I did NOT want to see that! I wanted everything to be cut and dried, black and white, right and wrong! And it *was* as far as whether or not he was *guilty* of sin! But there are nuances and needs that certainly played into whether or not he was *susceptible* to temptation. I had to face the fact that I was not meeting Tracy's needs, so he was left vulnerable.

I'm not talking about physical needs, because those were always met. He had a fairly clean house, meals on the table, physical intimacy, and so on. But I was doing nothing to meet his need for respect, which is a man's greatest need from other people. Instead, I belittled and berated him at every turn. I had to face the fact that *I* was the one the Lord had provided to help meet my husband's need for acceptance and respect, and I had failed miserably to do so. It didn't make Tracy's actions okay, but it made them understandable. I had left him vulnerable to attack from the enemy, and it was time that I admitted the part I played in that, difficult though it was for me to do so.

Remember, forgiveness does not mean that what the offender did was okay! Paul dealt with a man from the Corinthian church who was guilty of having sex with his father's wife. The punishment was severe! The church was instructed to expel the man, to "turn him over to Satan" for a time so he would be saved (1 Corinthians 5:1-5). Later, in another letter to the Corinthian church, Paul told them that the man had suffered enough and that it was time to restore him. He was to be forgiven and comforted (2 Corinthians 2:5-8). Satan is the one who wants us divided and devouring one another. Sinners—both the saved and the unsaved—need to know that sin is utterly detestable and unacceptable, but that they are still loved and can be both forgiven and cleansed.

There were times when I would panic and wonder if Tracy was really being faithful or honest with me. It took time to work through that and get past it in my own thinking. I had to trust that if he weren't being sincere, God would deal with him and bring it out into the open. But love demanded that I go past that—that I also pray for his holiness and walk with God, not just trust he'd be judged if he wasn't living right!

Restoration is a beautiful thing, and the Lord promises that He will make everything beautiful in His time. How thankful I am for waiting instead of divorcing Tracy when I first learned of his sin! The Lord brought us through that terrible time, and now we are experiencing a love that is far greater than anything we could have hoped for before the pain! It isn't based on feelings, but rather on mutual realization of our own neediness and obedience to the Lord. It is unconditional. And the nice thing is that often the romantic feelings and chemistry are also there to add extra blessing. Hope can be restored; I am living proof!

So we see that God's Word does say we *can* divorce if there has been unfaithfulness, but it doesn't say we have to or that it's the best plan. If you are the victim of betrayal of this sort, ask the Lord what is best for you and your children, if you have any. He truly wants the very best for you, and He is not out to make you miserable! He can show you what to do!

If your husband had an affair, and it was a one-time thing, that is a different story from a situation where the spouse is addicted to sex or women and has repeatedly broken his covenant with you. You also want to consider whether or not he has any intention of changing, or if he prefers to maintain his lifestyle this way. You might be able to find out the root cause of his infidelity, and that can help determine whether or not he is likely to change the pattern of behavior. You do have to think about the possibility of contracting a sexually transmitted disease if your husband won't stop his affairs. (It only takes ONE sexual encounter with an infected person to become infected yourself, so that is definitely a factor to consider.)

If your spouse has engaged in homosexual activities, that is another set of circumstances altogether. It is possible to overcome homosexuality, but it is not easy—certainly not something to tackle alone! This sin was punishable by death in the Old Testament, and it certainly would be considered unfaithfulness, so you are within your "rights" to terminate the marriage. Once again, ask the Lord what is best for your individual case. Is there a repentant heart? A desire for change?

Honesty? We have close friends who divorced over that very issue, and they were apart for fifteen years, but now they have remarried each other again. They would be the first to admit, though, that the road has not always been easy.

According to numerous studies on the subject, if your spouse has molested his own flesh and blood child(ren), he is an extremely depraved individual with very little hope for change. That crosses a line that most psychologists do not believe a person can recover from. Anything is possible with Jesus, but that is a situation that has not only no guarantees, but very little chance for a normal life or rebuilding trust. Men who molest other people's children have a better chance of recovery and change than those who violate their birth children, but again, discovering the motivation behind the sin is crucial to the healing process.

Of course, there are also the situations that involve abuse, alcoholism, or addictions of other natures. There is a time for being separated and even divorcing. I am not suggesting that I am an authority on any of these situations! I believe it must be decided after much prayer and counseling from a godly pastor or counselor who knows what God's Word has to say on the subject. I also believe a time of separation can be tried first to give the offender a chance to mend his or her ways. Change IS possible! But it is not guaranteed in any circumstances. The safety of the threatened spouse and children involved is always first and foremost!

Willingness on the part of the offenders to be honest about their sin in any of these situations is an absolute must before change can occur. But even then, it is between you and the Lord as to whether or not you can or should continue in the relationship. Forgiveness is a must; we know that unless we forgive, we will not be forgiven, and we will suffer the consequences in every area. But that does not necessarily mean that we have to go back into the situation, even if the offender promises he has changed or that he wants to. The Lord is willing to show you what is best for you and your family when the circumstances are so intense.

So many Christians are set on NO divorce, and they quote the sentiment found in Malachi 2:16: "God hates divorce." Yes, He does because He realizes how much it hurts us! But we must realize that there are also *other* things that He hates just as much! He hates child molestation. Homosexuality. Violence. And so on.

Just realize that the majority of divorces in our nation are NOT over these issues. It is most often simply the result of selfishness and unforgiveness on the part of both parties involved. That is something that grieves the Lord and scars the children of our nation. There is hope for these situations! If you have been unhappy, if you're separated, or if you're considering a divorce, please read the following studies very carefully.

According to a study reported on the 700 Club on July 11, 2002, couples who are unhappily married are better off to stay married rather than divorce. The study showed that five years later, those who stayed married ended up happier than those who decided to divorce.

The April 17, 2001, printing of Agape Press has an article written by Randall Murphee titled "Family Therapist Cites Scars of Divorce on Children." He quotes Dr. Robert N. Crankshaw, who worked nine years as an elementary school counselor, eight years as a marriage and family therapist, and at the time of the article had been director of counseling services at Palmer Home for Children in Columbus, Mississippi, for eleven years. His studies conclude without question that there are long-term scars from divorce. His three decades of counseling have convinced him that divorce has a much more critical impact on children than our culture leads us to believe. He cites that even when they appear to be well-adjusted, there is still a higher incidence of "distractions, lower grades at school, acting up in school, and more depression." And the crucial factor he has discovered is that even when children seem to be coping and adjusting to the divorce, their issues show up later when they are adults. Their ability to trust and bond is affected, as well as "their view of marriage, their fear of losing their security, [and] their fear of losing loving relationships."

Dr. Crenshaw says that even though children are superficially resilient, "the pop psychology premise that a child is better off with one 'happy' parent than with two 'unhappy' parents is just not valid." He also states that the scars from divorce do not heal. This suggests that perhaps we as a nation need to consider the needs of our children more carefully before rushing to divorce court.

Americans need to get reacquainted with the word commitment. I know very well how painful a marriage without love can be, because I've lived through one! But I've also lived on the other side of that scenario, finding that love can be learned! I've discovered that love is actually something you DO, not an emotion you feel. Yet when you do loving things, your feelings amazingly are changed over time. I feel romantically in love with Tracy—most days! But on the days when I don't, our commitment and the knowledge that God blesses obedience carry me through until the feelings return.

To those of you who are fellow believers, I am making an appeal. Titus 2:3-5 tells us that the older women need to teach the younger women to love their husbands and be subject to them so that God's Word will not be maligned. The King James version uses the word *blasphemed* instead of maligned. Truth be told, the world is looking at our marriages and lives today and saying that they don't want anything to do with Christianity because our lives are no different from theirs! This should not be! We are so selfish that we aren't showing how very big and good our God really is. One day we will stand before the Lord, and we should not think that we will be blameless for those who have rejected the Gospel message because of the messes we've made of our lives!

If you are already divorced, please do not allow these words to discourage you or heap condemnation on you. Perhaps the divorce was not your choice, but your husband is the one who insisted on it. You can't control that. I Corinthians 7:15 tells us that if the unbeliever leaves, we should let him do so, and the believer in the situation is not bound by such circumstances. The Lord wants us to live in peace. Even if your husband is supposedly a Christian, but he isn't living like a believer in Jesus, then there is not much you can do to hold him except honor him and pray for him. If he is still intent on leaving, don't resist him.

If you already were divorced, and it was your own decision, and now you realize you didn't have a biblical reason for the divorce, you will need to work through the issues involved. For instance, if you want to live a godly life that is pleasing to God, you will not remarry in this situation; that would be committing adultery. You might think that's not fair! You might wish you had hurried up and been remarried before you knew the truth! You might feel tempted to go ahead and find a spouse, trusting that God will just forgive you after the fact. He can and does forgive any sin, including adultery, but that kind of thinking misses the point. It's still presuming that God's law doesn't have your best interest at heart and that the only way to find fulfillment is with a new partner. Neither is true! His laws were given out of His love for us. He knows how much we'll hurt ourselves living outside of them. And *He* is waiting to fulfill us Himself!

You will have consequences, often quite painful, but it isn't the end of the world. You can still find hope, forgiveness, and the ability to rebuild a good life, perhaps even finding that you now have the time to serve the needs of others. Find out what went wrong. Be willing to see how you contributed to the problems. Don't play the blame game and refuse responsibility for your part in it, if any. Let Jesus truly begin to meet your needs so that you will be whole. Otherwise, you will continue to look for another *person* to complete you.

And at the beginning of a new relationship, it seems the other person DOES complete you like no one else ever has before! But as time takes its toll, you start to see familiar patterns of behavior in yourself. Negative emotions show up and take their toll. Fighting ensues and escalates. If you don't deal with the issues that got you into trouble in the first place, they will repeat themselves in your life and the lives of those you love.

If you have not remarried and neither has your ex, please consider a reconciliation. Read *Daughters of Sarah* and ask the Lord to show you if there are areas where you need to repent (turn around and do things differently). See if the Lord might lead you to a restoration that is beyond anything you could have hoped for!

If one or both of you have already remarried someone else, just realize that if you *were* wrong to divorce, you can ask the Lord to forgive you and help you learn His principles for your new marriage. We have very close friends who went through a difficult time of questioning. He was divorced when they married, and when they realized that he was committing adultery with his new wife, they wondered if *they* should also divorce so he could try to reconcile with his first wife. NO! That would be tearing up more lives all over again! They realized they just had to confess the sin to the Lord and trust Him to forgive them and go on.

One of my former students left her husband. They have two small children. I was standing in line with her at a wedding reception for one of her cousins, and she made the comment to me that she didn't intend to ever be married again. My heart ached for her. She was planning to have a tummy tuck, because her *tiny* bulge "interfered with her daily life." She was already totally gorgeous and didn't need any outside interference to make her more beautiful! But her lifestyle choices forced her to try to impress men continuously instead of resting in the security that comes from years of loving and being loved by the same person.

There are other single and divorced women who intend to stay single, and for some, a single life is the best choice. But there are also great benefits for married women, so if the decision to remain single is merely due to the pain you've experienced, it is worth working through those issues. According to research, we married women are healthier physically, mentally, and emotionally than unmarried women. We have fewer physical health problems and live longer than singles. A study of seventeen nations revealed that married couples are far happier than singles, couples living together, and divorcees.

Abuse rates are also lower among married women; the vast majority of abuse/domestic violence incidents are between boyfriends and girlfriends, not husbands and wives. Married women are more than three times less likely to be physically assaulted than single women.

Married couples enjoy more physically and emotionally satisfying sex than unmarried partners, according to the most authoritative study of sexual behavior in the United States, conducted at the University of Chicago! Marriage is a good thing!

When Scripture tells us that Abraham "knew" his wife, it speaks of the kind of relationship that comes with living with the same person for many years and physically loving her during that time. Eventually you don't even have to always say what you need or want—or what pleases you. The other person just knows what your subtle signals mean and knows how to meet those needs.

Divorce is not the unpardonable sin, and neither is adultery. But what a mess they leave in their wake! Neither should be taken lightly! Let the Lord heal you and love you and meet your needs!

10. There's a Draft in the Castle (An overdraft, that is!)

It is so easy to believe that if we were wealthy, our marriages would be much happier! We think that problems would disappear, but actually, wealth can create a whole new set of problems for us to deal with! God loves to bless His people, but He also knows whether or not we can handle wealth. We SHOW Him by how faithful we are with a little; if He can trust us with that, then He can "safely" increase it.

When we have financial difficulties, it is important to get to the root of the trouble, just as we need to in other areas of marriage. Is it a lack of discipline—spending without realizing the limitations on the budget? Laziness—unwillingness to work hard enough to meet the obligations? Greed—feeling the need for more and more without ever being satisfied? Pride—wanting to look as good or better than our peers or what we see portrayed in the movies? This is only a partial list of root causes that can contribute to the material mess.

Of course, sometimes there are factors that we feel we have little or no control over that add to the struggles: lack of education, having a larger family than we'd planned for, unexpected high medical expenses, and so on. While some people look at challenges like those and begin to figure out how to find an answer, others feel trapped in the socio-economic lifestyle they grew up in, and they can't see a way out.

It has been said that financial woes cause a huge percent of the breakups of marriage in the United States. Personal bankruptcies have skyrocketed, and credit card debt enslaves almost every family. It is rare to find a couple that isn't thousands of dollars in debt to credit card companies. In fact, in the United States, credit card and installment debt have increased 30% in just two years at the turn of the century. It tops over $1 trillion dollars! I got an e-mail from "Debt Free" ("Debt Free" provenstrategy@anmail.com) on February 24, 2001, that adds the following statistics:

> 96% of all Americans will retire financially dependent on the government, family or charity. On average, the typical credit card purchase is 112% higher than if using cash. The average consumer takes 23 years and pays 2.4 to 3 times what they owe to pay back their debt. Only 2% of homes in America are paid for. 50% to 70% of your minimum monthly payments only pays the

interest on most credit card accounts. The median amount of total debt owed was $23,400 in 1995 and jumped to $33,300 in 1998. High credit card balances can disqualify you from obtaining a mortgage or car loan. From March 1997 to March 1998, 1,370,490 people filed for personal bankruptcy, or 3,754 people per day. Over 40% of US families spend more than they earn. The average household has four credit cards with balances around $4,800. Making the minimum payment at 18% interest, it will take nearly 40 years to pay off the balance and you will have paid a total of nearly $16,000. 85% of Americans have a true net worth of $250. 60% of adults in America have given no thought to retirement planning. 89% of all divorces are caused by money problems. For every person and organization who uses debt wisely, 10 people misuse it. People in debt have higher rates of health problems, ignore needed medical, dental, & chiropractic work. American's owe $4.5 trillion on their home mortgages, up from $2.5 trillion a decade ago. [This could well be because mortgagers are allowing people to refinance their homes, adding other debts to the balance, such as credit cards and cars, postponing their ability to pay off the houses. They owe] $1.4 trillion on their cars, plastic and student loans, up from $811 billion in 1990. From 1992 to 1999 card issuers increased credit lines more than four times. From $499 billion to more than $2.11 trillion, which breaks down to almost $21,000 per household. People have been filing for protection from creditors at the rate of more than 1 million a year since 1996, up fourfold since 1979. As of yearend in 1999, American consumers have racked up $462 billion in bank credit card debt and $88 billion in retail (store, gas, etc.) credit card debt.

"Debt Free" took these statistics from many sources, including the US Department of Health & Human Services, North American Marketing, and *Forbes*, to name a few. The numbers are sobering!

I saw Howard Dayton on the 700 Club on October 16, 2003. He is the CEO of Crown Financial Ministries. He said that there have been 1.6 million bankruptcies in the U.S. this year. That's one out of every sixty-nine families! He also said that if the rate of bankruptcies continues at its current pace, one in seven families will be bankrupt in ten more years! I don't know about you, but that SCARES me!

Tracy and I have not been immune to the temptation to spend more than we make, sad to say. In fact, it is a continual battle—sometimes fought within and sometimes fought with each other! The stresses of overspending definitely affect marital harmony! We are often unaware of the snowball effect on our society at large, as well, because individuals don't pay, so businesses go under, so there's more unemployment, and on it goes.

If Christians are as guilty as the rest of the world, who is funding missions? II Timothy 3:1-5 states,

> *"But mark this: There will be terrible times in the last days. People will be lovers of themselves, lovers of money, boastful, proud, abusive, disobedient to their parents, ungrateful, unholy, without love, unforgiving, slanderous, without self-control, brutal, not lovers of the good, treacherous, rash, conceited, lovers of pleasure rather than lovers of God—having a form of godliness but denying its power. Have nothing to do with them."*

In 1 Timothy 6:6-12, 17-19, Paul explains,

> *"But godliness with contentment is great gain. For we brought nothing into the world, and we can take nothing out of it. But if we have food and clothing, we will be content with that. People who want to get rich fall into temptation and a trap and into many foolish and harmful desires that plunge men into ruin and destruction. For the love of money is a root of all kinds of evil. Some people, eager for money, have wandered from the faith and pierced themselves with many griefs. But you, man of God, flee from all this, and pursue righteousness, godliness, faith, love, endurance and gentleness. Fight the good fight of the faith . . . . Command those who are rich in this present world not to be arrogant nor to put their hope in wealth, which is so uncertain, but to put their hope in God, who richly provides us with everything for our enjoyment. Command them to do good, to be rich in good deeds, and to be generous and willing to share. In this way they will lay up treasure for themselves as a firm foundation for the coming age, so that they may take hold of the life that is truly life."*

So many Americans LIVE for their paychecks and what they can purchase with them. Paul told Timothy there was something else to pursue! The focus of our lives is to know, love, and serve God, Who really does want to bless us. The truth is, we in America—even those who are unemployed or who live paycheck to paycheck—are in the top 8% wealthiest people in the world! Yet it doesn't seem to be enough to satisfy us, because we are trying to fill a spiritual need with something temporary. It can't be done!

When Tracy and I first married, I was "in charge" of the budget, and we had decided I would stay home instead of working at a paying job. Still, I had school loans and some consumer debt to pay off, so there was NO extra. Tracy and I would get into huge fights if he so much as bought a Pepsi! We simply couldn't afford it if we were going to pay our bills on time!

Couples often have different views of money, based on their experiences growing up and their personalities. Tracy and I were no different. As the oldest of six children whose father was a truck driver and alcoholic for many of my growing up years, I had learned to be frugal. Tracy, on the other hand, was the youngest of two children, and both of his parents worked. They were not wealthy, by any means, but he could always get whatever he needed, and usually even what he wanted.

Talk about mixing water with oil! We had a lot to overcome in this area! Still, we based our budget on godly principles from the very beginning, especially as relating to tithing. No matter how much or how little we had, we always gave the Lord at least ten percent of our income. We knew that He would provide for all of our needs as we looked to Him, and He has been faithful to us through the years!

I know that some people believe tithing is an Old Testament principle, but I urge you to read the Book for yourself! Jesus taught that where a person's treasure is, there his heart will also be! He also said that a person can't serve both God and money! I know one pastor who won't even counsel with people who don't tithe! His attitude is that if they aren't tithing, God doesn't have their hearts! Their treasure isn't going to the Kingdom! So if God doesn't have their hearts, this pastor feels that even if he counseled with them until he was blue in the face, nothing he said would make a difference until they really gave their hearts to the Lord!

Now I'm not saying that if you aren't tithing, you aren't fully devoted to the Lord. I know there could be many circumstances that would hinder your ability to give God the tithe. Perhaps you have stretched yourself too far with credit card debt. Perhaps you've had a business deal that has gone sour. Maybe your husband doesn't see the need to tithe. Those are personal matters between each family and the Lord! I just know from my experience and others I've heard share through the years that you can't out-give God! He blesses generosity!

Genevieve White believes that if the husband doesn't want to tithe, the wife should not do it behind his back or against his wishes! Good advice! Who is the head of the home? You can pray for your husband to realize the truth of this teaching and to know the freedom that comes from giving, but unless he sees it or okay's it, I don't believe God would want it from you! The truth is, God doesn't need your money! As the old chorus goes, "He owns the cattle on a thousand hills!" He wants your heart! He might be asking you to trust Him about your spouse more than your tithe!

I do believe that if it's possible and you have your husband's agreement, you should try to work towards tithing, though. In Malachi we learn that withholding the tithe is robbing God and we'll find that we don't even know where the money is going. It will seem our purses have holes in them! But God will bless us if we give with a pure motive!

Even if funds are tight, the tithe comes off the top. Many times in our younger years, we didn't have enough money to do everything we needed to do, but we would go ahead and tithe in faith to the Lord. We NEVER had to pay a bill late because of our tithing! We never missed a meal! True, we didn't eat steak, but too much meat is bad for you, anyway, right?! Ha!

I have to share what happened to us when we had our three birth children, two teen-aged girls for whom we were legal guardians, and four college-aged young men living with us! Tracy was the only one who was working steadily and contributing to the bills, so it did get tight at times. During one particularly lean time, I was serving popcorn for supper on Sunday nights. I felt SO guilty about it, worrying about poor nutrition.

What is funny about that situation is that years later, the girls told me that one of their favorite memories of our time at that house was the Sunday night popcorn meals! They would throw popcorn into the air and catch it with their mouths. Or they'd see how many pieces of popcorn they could get into their mouths at once. They made a game out of it and totally enjoyed that time together! They still laughed about it years later! Isn't that just like the Lord, to take something that we consider a hardship and turn it into a precious memory? He is SO good!

Another experience during that time was one evening when it was time to start cooking dinner, but I had absolutely nothing to cook. This time, I knew I needed real food, because even though they didn't work enough to contribute to the budget, most of the fellows were working manual labor and the older children were in school. Nutrition was important to fuel their bodies to keep doing their best. I had prayed, but I had not told another soul about our predicament. Just when I was starting to really wonder where supper was going to come from, the front door bell rang. It was a woman from our church—and not one who had a lot to spare—but she and her husband were carrying in sack after sack of groceries for us! The Lord had laid us on her heart, so she was obedient, and we ate well for several meals! He is faithful!

Again, this doesn't mean you should never share with others what your needs are—quite to the contrary, the Word tells us to bear one another's burdens, and we can't do that if we don't know what they are. But in this particular situation, I really didn't feel I was supposed to ask for help. Of course, if I'd known then what I know now, I'd have asked Tracy what to do, and I'd have been resting much more about the outcome! The Lord is so good to just take us where we are, though! In those days, it was a faith walk to simply trust Him to supply! Now, it's a faith walk for me to trust He can supply through my husband!

If the Lord changed us completely the day we invited Him into our lives, none of us would be able to bear it! We can't even begin to imagine how much junk is in us, needing His touch and teaching and requiring our surrender! In fact, while our son Benjamin was in South Africa doing mission work, we needed to help raise support for his training back in the states for the coming year. I went through our house with a vengeance and set aside truckloads of stuff for a huge garage sale for him. You already know how I cling to things and how hard it is for me to let go, so this was really a big step! But I was facing that issue and choosing to part with things I really liked, all for the "cause"! I have to admit, I was feeling pretty good about my ability to sacrifice for the furthering of the Kingdom of God!

Not long afterwards, though, I read a Scripture that stunned me. I'd read it many times before, but now it held real impact. It is found in Luke 6:29: "If someone takes your cloak, do not stop him from taking your tunic." If I had only two upper garments like this, would I even be willing to part with one of them? Much less *both* of them? Honestly, probably not! Obviously there's still room for lots of growth in me!

So we just walk with God and take it one step at a time, being changed from one degree of glory to the next. Perhaps He's asking you to take a step of faith where your finances are concerned. Maybe He is asking you to begin to trust Him to meet your needs as you tithe. Or it might be that He's asking you to stop using a credit card and begin to pray for Him to provide for your needs as you lower your standards and live within your means! (Ouch!) He has promised that if we are seeking His Kingdom first, He will provide for us better than the sparrows and clothe us better than the lilies! (Matthew 6:25-34) King David tells us in Psalm 37:25 that he's never seen the righteous forsaken or God's children begging bread! Amen!

Rather than fighting with each other about finances, let's give this area to the Lord and let Him sanctify it, setting it apart for holy use in our lives and those around us! Need is simply an opportunity to see God move on our behalf! Instead of meeting our own needs with a charge card or stressing out, we can walk the exciting faith walk of letting Him lead us and take care of us!

Tracy and I took a huge step of faith this past summer. I began to sense in the spring that the Lord wanted me to stay home instead of teaching. As much as I love my students and teaching, I just couldn't spread myself far enough to do a good job at school while also doing a good job parenting AND finishing this book. I was sensing that the Lord wanted me to refocus again on ministering to women. We knew that financially it would be an adjustment; not only would we lose my contribution to the budget, but we would also have to add tuition to our kids' Christian school back into the budget. It would be a difference of over $2,000 a month. Tracy agreed to pray about it and I warned my administrator that he would probably want to start keeping his eyes open for someone to replace me.

One of the things the Lord showed me was again a portion of Scripture that I'd read many times before. It's found in Mark's account of Jesus feeding the 5,000. Before that miracle, Jesus had sent out the twelve apostles to minister, and they had returned to Him with many stories of what had happened as they had healed the sick and cast out demons. Yet they were tired and hungry, so He told them to go with Him to a quiet place where they could rest.

The crowds figured out where they were headed, though, and were waiting for Jesus and his disciples when they arrived. Jesus was moved with compassion on the crowds, because they were like sheep without a shepherd. So He took the time to teach them. It started getting pretty late, so the twelve approached Jesus and asked if they could send the people away to the nearby villages to purchase food. Jesus' answer surprised them—He told THEM to feed the crowds! Now they were upset! They asked Him if He expected them to spend eight months' wages to feed so many people. They were already hungry and tired themselves, and it seemed He didn't really care about their needs. But we know how the story goes; He asked them to bring what they had, and He fed over 5,000 men, plus their wives and children, with only two fish and five loaves of bread.

The thing that I had never noticed as significant before was the baskets that were picked up afterwards: exactly twelve baskets of leftovers were filled after all those people had had their fill, including the disciples. Twelve apostles, twelve baskets. Coincidence? I don't believe so! I think Jesus was making a point to His followers, that if they would simply be obedient to Him and trust Him, even if they had to keep serving occasionally when they'd rather rest, He would still take care of them individually. He didn't send home a full basket with every person who was there; there were only the twelve baskets to show His disciples He knew their needs and cared about them.

The message to me was so clear! If I would just be obedient to the Lord and begin to minister to women like He was asking of me, then He would take care of our needs. We would have enough. We have found that to be true thus far, sometimes through amazing events. Even more importantly, women have actually been showing up at my front door! Some who need prayer, some who need advice, some who just need a listening ear. That sure wasn't happening when I was teaching! And it seems that the emotional needs of our children are being met far better, as well. I know I'm walking in a level of peace and expectancy that I haven't had for a long, long time. The Lord is restoring me in many ways, and all of my family receives the benefit along with me.

I'm not telling you to quit your job! That's between you, your husband, and the Lord! I'm just letting you know that He really is our ultimate Provider. If we will be faithful, He will bless us and take care of us. If you're trapped in credit card debt and overspending, let Him show you the way out. Find a counselor who specializes in that area, and begin to let Jesus be Lord of your finances. It is one powerful way to let Him know He is also Lord of your heart.

From a practical standpoint, it is also wise to begin to make a plan for how things will be different in the future. We have to change the way we look at money and material possessions if we hope to turn things around. The first step is to submit your finances to the Lord. If you've sinned in your attitudes towards money and things, confess that and ask the

Lord to help you. We know that the money and stuff can't really fulfill us, and it hurts our marriages in more ways than one. We might make our husbands feel inadequate if we are never satisfied! Begin to show the Lord that He means more to you than things and back your words up with action by starting to tithe. If you can't do the full 10%, then start someplace and work towards complete obedience.

Next, stop overspending! If there isn't enough money, don't use a credit card to go ahead and buy what you want! Most financial planners say that your house is really the only good debt. Cars decrease in value the minute you drive them off the lot, while houses normally become more valuable with time. So work towards living within a budget that does NOT include buying on credit. Learn to buy used at garage sales and thrift stores. For many years, we have clothed our large family this way with neat, clean, in-style fashions at a fraction of the retail price! It can be exciting to see how the Lord provides instead of meeting your own needs on credit!

As a couple, come up with a written budget that is workable, then stick to it! Discipline yourself to say no to your desires if there isn't money budgeted for the expenditure. You will enjoy things much more if you are able to buy them outright instead of using plastic to obtain them. Be sure to figure out how to reduce your debt, too. The pressure will be off.

Some Christians ask if they should file bankruptcy, and in most cases, I would say no. If you owe, you make good on your word to pay. Get a second job, do without, and form a plan. Most creditors will work with you on lower monthly payments as long as you are paying something. Take responsibility for your overspending and poor planning. Make it right. You will build respect for yourself and from others.

Withstand the temptation to refinance and consolidate your debts over and over and over. Sometimes it's a good plan to refinance for a lower interest rate, but don't do it just so you can spend more! Keep paying the amount you had already budgeted so you can pay off the debt earlier! Debt elimination should be the goal of every American! The "have now, pay later " mentality needs to be shot!

Sell things you no longer need or use. Apply the proceeds to debt reduction.

Start making a plan for your retirement. The economy has changed, and our trust must not be in our jobs or investments. But we can research other options that might be a better way of producing our primary incomes while allowing us to invest and save. Having a "Plan B" in place is also a good idea, considering the sad economic trends we have seen in the last two decades.

Marketing trends are changing, like they do every ten to twenty years, and now one-to-one marketing seems to be the trend of the future, along with mass customization. If these terms are unfamiliar and you are interested in knowing where the next high incomes will be found, get on the Internet and start plugging in some of these terms. Read *The Next Trillion* by Paul Zane Pilzer or other books on the topic. It is fascinating the way people can indicate what direction marketing is headed so we can get onboard! Tracy and I have found a business that uses these techniques of marketing and we are quite pleased with the income produced for the amount of time we spend. It is allowing us to begin to build income that will eventually outgrow his current income, as well as build towards our retirement.

Realize that as the economy changes, so do methods for gaining wealth. It used to be that to make a good living, a person in America needed to get a good education, then land a job in corporate America and stay with the company till retirement. Obviously that is no longer the case! So we need to quit making our plans as though it were! That small 4 - 5% of people who are ready for retirement and are financially fit by that stage of life almost all own their own businesses! Since most of us can't run out and buy a franchise to McDonald's to ensure future income, we need to research other possibilities and do our homework so we can position ourselves for future economic health.

I also recommend that you read materials that will help you change the way you perceive money, such as *Rich Dad, Poor Dad* or *Cash Flow Quadrant* both by Robert Kiyosaki. More importantly, how about the Bible? Did you know it references money more than heaven? It does! There are 2,350 verses in the Bible about financial principles, and 15% of everything Jesus said when He was here on earth was about money! The Lord wants us to understand it and use it as a tool, not be bound by it. The Bible doesn't tell us that money is evil; just loving it is! My pastor says it's okay to have things as long as the things don't have you! Would you be able to part with your stuff if that's what the Lord asked of you?

I sure want to be, even though I never considered myself great missionary material! The Lord let me know recently to quit making excuses for my pickiness about food and dislike of heat and bugs, etc.! He wants me to be willing to go where He says go and to quit holding onto the stuff that ties us down where we are! Two of my children feel called to missions and I want to help support them, sending them wherever the Lord calls. A willingness to walk away from my "stuff" if the Lord calls me to do so isn't enough; I also want to be in a financial position to do so! That's where getting out of debt comes in!

Anyway, money can be a blessing or a curse, both the abundance of it and the lack thereof. My attitude is that life is short and we want to reach as many people for Jesus as possible; if money or stuff will help with that, then I want some more of it.

11. The Middle Ages (or "The Old Gray Mare, She Ain't What She Used to Be!")

Okay, maybe the title should be that the old gray NAG, she ain't what she used to be! If, like me, you have reached those delightful years called middle age, you will have already discovered that things have changed physically! My health is not what it was when I was twenty! Neither is my body shape or metabolism! If you haven't reached middle age yet, read on, anyway, because you will! Either way, I'm going to broach the subject of three things that make even the most composed and refined of us gals sweat—hormones, exercise, and weight. I know, it would be cutesy to come up with an acronym for those words, such as H.E.W., but all that makes me think of is hewing out my own grave—because I'd rather die than actually deal with these issues.

Sad to say, that is exactly what will happen if they are left undealt with, so I guess I'd better just jump in. (Oh, did I say *jump*? I didn't mean that!)

Some people say that we can't blame our crankiness on our hormones, and there is some truth to that! Yet there is also a lot of truth to the fact that those hormones really do test our ability to be nice sometimes! Christian comedian Mark Lowery has a story about not looking, feeling, or even smelling like a Christian early in the morning, but if he were to throw in some estrogen issues with that, he'd really know what a struggle it is to keep the faith under duress!

True, we are to walk in the Spirit all the time, even during PMS, our periods, pregnancy, pre-menopause, actual menopause, and post-menopause! Anyone who says the highs and lows of our hormones during those times can't ever affect that challenge, though, has never been through it!

In my journal in October of 2000, I wrote that false submission is doing it outwardly without a true heart agreement. "I've been feeling so yucky and cranky that I can't even tell where my heart is, but Lord, I WANT to do what is right! Please change me inwardly for the long haul!" This was during a time when I was taking birth control pills to try to regulate my periods while waiting for my hysterectomy. It didn't help with the periods, and it made me almost crazy while waiting! Had the same effect on my family!

Later that month I wrote, "I'm so cranky in general and HATE being on the pill for that reason. I want to be sweet and loving and gentle and patient and kind—all fruits of Your Spirit (well, I don't know about the sweet—ha!). But I'm wound up and edgy on this medication. I hate it! Please help me!"

In November, I wrote "I'm still having trouble bleeding—too much and at the wrong time. Ugh. The pill *isn't* controlling it, but I have acne, edginess, weight gain, and a yeast infection from it!! Ugh!"

Even worse was some years earlier while we were trying to conceive a baby, and my obstetrician put me on a drug called Chlomid. He wanted to see if this would help me maintain a pregnancy. It did help me conceive, but I miscarried four more times while on it! What it did to my hormones was another story. Cranky doesn't even begin to paint a picture of what I was like. I was a WITCH! I screamed at everyone! I griped continuously! I even hit someone! That was not my normal behavior, but it changed who I was! It was a nightmare! Nobody can convince me that hormones don't affect our behavior, especially when they are drug-induced.

So what are we to do? Some husbands have suggested locking ourselves in the bathrooms for several weeks at a time, but there isn't enough Calgon in the universe to take care of that scenario! Besides, we all know chocolate is not eaten best in the bathroom, and it's a sure necessity during those times of duress!

I really don't have any easy answers. Since the time of my hysterectomy, I've discovered some herbs that do wonders for all kinds of female hormonal issues. Wish I'd known about them way back then! I know that doctors also encourage exercise and rest and good nutrition to help us through. (I don't know what they suggest for our husbands and children!) Other than those suggestions, I can only say that we need to prepare ourselves spiritually for those times of life, prepare our husbands and families with enough information to help them be patient with us, and then give ourselves grace. We KNOW that monster coming through is NOT the real us! If it is a serious enough issue to really affect relationships, then it's worth a trip to the doctor or a visit to the Internet for more information on what can be done to lessen symptoms. I'd be happy to share what I've learned, as well.

Meanwhile, what about exercise? I hate to sweat! I hate to ache! The only exercise I like is swimming, and in Kansas, that is definitely only a summer sport! So do I ask the Lord for the money to put in an indoor-outdoor pool in the back yard or beg Him to move me to Florida? Who has time for the YMCA? If they'd move it next door and let me use it between 11:00 P.M. and 3:00 A.M., then it might work out! Oh, did I just use the words work and out together? Yikes! Run! Oh, no! Now I said run! I'd better back track—oops, there's the word track! I can't seem to get away from it! Reminders of exercise are surrounding me!

Truth is, we need to "move it" for health's sake. I like music, so I sometimes "Sweat to the Oldies" with Richard Simmons. Variety can be helpful, too, switching from a video to walking to swimming or bicycling. It's also encouraging to be accountable or do our exercising with a group of others who care. Just making simple adjustments can help over time, too, such as parking further away from the door at the department store or taking the stairs instead of the elevator. [Note: for safety reasons, never use a dark stairwell in an isolated area alone even if you DO want to slenderize your thunder thighs!] Getting up to get our own supplies instead of sending our kids for them comes to mind, too! HA! Just anything that will help us move around more than we are currently. We'll feel better and teach our children well and live longer! Not to mention the side benefit of looking better, too!

Of course, most of us don't want to use the word "around" when we're talking about this topic, either—it could be a description of our body shape! Weight is an issue that plagues American women. It's not just the over-forty crowd who are concerned, either; even the young girls fret over their figures. We are either overweight or anorexic! We worry about our weight, try to diet, berate ourselves for not exercising, take weight loss pills, and deny ourselves—only to find that we are far from healthy in this area.

Do you remember when you used to buy a pair of blue jeans because you felt good in them? Since you *looked* good, you *felt* good, and you were willing to pay any amount of your hard-earned babysitting or waitressing money to have that denim that would send you out of the door in style!

Well, I still buy blue jeans that make me feel good! Only now it's because they have an elastic waist! Ha! I don't want them to cut in too deeply to keep me from feeling like I can have that piece of chocolate cake! Or that mocha almond fudge ice cream! Double dip! Seriously, I don't *really* buy elastic waist jeans; having my jeans too tight in the waist is a link to reality for me! Keeps me motivated to DO something when I'm gaining!

Weight is an issue most of us will face, either because we have too much of it or too little. The majority of us have too much, sad to say. We all know how society has contributed to our obsession with it, because the media paints a false image of women, creating a standard impossible to live up to. And the hysterical thing is, men get by with continuing to wear the same size pants they wore in puberty; they just let their bellies hang over the tops of their jeans! Only we women really feel the overwhelming pressure to conform!

We've heard our entire lives that we are what we eat. Well, our bodies might be, but WE are much more than that! Who we are *inside* is what matters. What others think of us isn't important—it's what we think of ourselves that is significant. It's what God thinks of us. Yet what others think *affects* us. What do we imagine is going on in their heads? That fat is a sign of laziness. That fat is a sign of an undisciplined life. That we are disgusting. That nobody would ever want us. And we think of reasons for our overeating: I eat because I'm depressed. I eat because I'm happy. I eat because I'm angry. I eat because I'm trying to fill a void. I eat because I had to clean my plate when I was a child. I eat because my mother made me feel guilty about the starving children in China. I eat because it's a social activity. I eat because it's part of my job to take people out. I eat because . . . you fill in the blanks.

But it's something that will lead us to an early grave if we don't get our eating under control. Again, sometimes just doing the simple things make such a difference. I gave up Pepsi, which was like an addict giving up drugs! My mouth still waters when I eat Mexican food and remember how good it tastes with that missing soda! I also quit drinking coffee except for special occasions, because I like it with cream and sugar and because it's really a diuretic that makes us dehydrated. And dehydration is something which our body often reads as hunger pangs instead of thirst! I've also given up eating a huge bowl of ice cream every evening for a snack!

I feel SO much better with these changes. Now I'm tackling a new area of trying to change the kinds of carbs I eat. We really DO need carbs for energy, contrary to some popular theories. The simple ones are SO delicious—white potatoes and rice and breads, potato chips, sugar, etc. But the complex are much better for us, so I'm trying to eat the red potatoes and brown rice and whole wheat grains and oatmeal in place of the white and bleached stuff. I'm buying baked corn tortilla chips for my homemade salsa, which I won't give up unless the Lord appears and demands it of me in an audible voice! Ha! (Actually, salsa is very good for you! Whew!) Scores of books have been written on the topic and hardly a day goes by without hearing something on a talk show or the news about diet, so getting the information isn't the problem; it's doing what we know. We must somehow consume fewer calories than we burn!

One thing that many people don't realize is that not getting enough rest is also a contributing factor to weight gain. In fact, being exhausted can affect our feelings of loneliness and depression. It's really important to be rested. On the other hand, loneliness and depression can make us more susceptible to exhaustion! So we need to be sure we're feeding our souls and spirits! Take time for friends, "play" more, do the "have-to's" early so the day is more flexible, read things you enjoy, and so on.

Stress also contributes to weight gain! And moms wrote the book on being overwhelmed! In fact, we usually think that moms have the hardest job on earth, and there is a lot of truth to that idea. Dads will have to give an account before God for what happened in their homes, so they have the greater responsibility, but moms are usually the ones with more to do than is possible to accomplish in any given day.

Busyness can make our lives insane! It can't please the Lord! I look back over journals from the time when Tracy was working nights and I was expecting Anna. It was a zoo while I was basically a single mother from Monday morning till Saturday afternoon! It was not healthful emotionally or physically or spiritually for any of us. We all suffered and there is still an element of consequences and loss to those years, especially for our son Nathan.

December 9, 1995 ***All*** *of us are too busy and since Ben & Justin missed school, they have tons of homework to make up. Jeri's been on everyone's nerves and I've totally lost my cool with her. Sara was given only three jobs—scrub 3rd floor bathroom, dust living room, and check laundry—none were accomplished correctly in five hours. Naturally she had to go to work, so couldn't do it later. Polly did Ashley's picking up for her instead of teaching Ashley to do it correctly. . . . Oh, I didn't write yesterday—was up at 5:38 A.M. to prepare for the 8th grade field trip to see "The Treasures of the Czars" in Topeka. Finally arrived home from trip & returning sitter, fed kids, dealt with puppies, did Christmas activity w/ kids, & prepared for bed. I'm* ***SO*** *sore today from the bus ride—the seats aren't made for expectant mamas.*

I understand that we're supposed to need others, but when I'm having a week like this past one when ***nobody*** *is following through, it really seems easier & less stressful just to do it all myself in the 1st place. I'm so* *frustrated. I'm sick of being a "single mom" most of the time. I don't know how we'll manage with a baby, too.*

December 15, 1995 Right now I need to know how to juggle all the "stuff" going on with my tremendous need for rest. Wednesday was **SO** *hard, esp. because Nathan was sick during the early hours (104.6 degree temp) and needed me. I had to be at the Ramada from 7 - 5, then took Ashley to the dr., kids shopping, home for a quick bite, and Ben's homework till past 11 P.M. There wasn't a minute for resting. Yesterday and today haven't been much better. I didn't even* **touch** *the laundry until last night (clear from Tues. afternoon!) and it becomes almost insurmountable in the winter if I miss a day. UGH! Too much going on.*

January 9, 1996 Ugh, what a day! I overslept (so did Nathan) so Doug's mom had to drive him in and Nathan was late to practice. I spent all morning at the dentist's with Justin and couldn't run my errands because the receptionist said the dr. wanted to talk to me (which he **didn't** *do until the end). This put me 1 ½ hrs. behind running errands. I finally got home & Sara called to say she had a bad pain in her right abdomen. Mr. Mitchell wanted to talk, too—said she was* **pale** *& really in pain. So the entire afternoon was spent in the doctor's office. The nurse wanted us to wait for lab results, which was a waste of time; they finally sent us home to wait for a* **call** *about results. Sara felt better so we went to her game. Of course, she started hurting again, so she didn't play after all (I could have stayed home and worked with Ben on HW. Instead we finished [well,* **quit**] *at a little after 11). He still needs to do his book report and study for history & science tests. Ugh. (I repeat.)*

I'm pooped but wanted to write for the sheer discipline of it. Now my lead is giving out so I'm quitting.

January 10, 1996 At last—a night when we didn't have to go anywhere and the kids are all getting to bed on time! I won't know what to DO if I actually get to bed before midnight! I might even feel human in the morning and decide to make breakfast! I might (dare I dream it?) **accomplish** *more than survival tomorrow!*

January 11, 1996 Well, I DID get to bed by 10:30, but I woke up at 4:30 A.M. and couldn't go back to sleep. I guess my body is used to only 6 hrs. sleep! I was able to make blueberry muffins, though, and start getting a little done this morning. I'm already feeling really sleepy—maybe a morning nap will be necessary today!

January 14, 1996 HOW can I be consistent? LIFE keeps happening to me! This time I came down with the flu Thurs. night—ran a fever 3 days and didn't even get out of bed except to go to the bathroom. Ugh. Now I'm playing "catch up" again—feeling totally unorganized and overwhelmed. ***HELP****! (Wonder who that is directed to. Wonder who it* **should** *be directed to. Wonder if I really can ask anyone—a real person. Wonder if I can just forget it all. Nope. Got to get on top of it all.)*

January 18, 1996 Another crazy day! We had a terrible winter storm w/ wind chill of -40°—didn't take the kids to school until this afternoon. Nathan had his best basketball game ever tonight against Little River—he scored 13 or 15 pts—we're not sure which. Tracy gave me the wrong directions, so I got to Little River late then learned they were playing in Windom. I missed the 1st 3 quarters!

Tomorrow will be another wild one, too. 9:30-awards assembly, then pick up Quentin & Riley [my nephews]. 11:30-Julie for lunch. 2:15-Dr. Cullan. 6:30-Sara's basketball game. Then Ben's slumber/ birthday party. Sometime in there I need to clean house, prepare food & snacks, do my Inc. stuff [music/record company I was working with], and pay attention to Tracy! Life is SO interesting!

Lord, please give me strength and joy in the little things.

January 21, 1996 I'm feeling so small up against all I need to do. Seems I have zero time to just be alone and recap or rest or plan or just BE. I NEED to get a grip on my obligations tomorrow. Lord, I'm asking You for help. I'm trusting You to help me find the balance . . . .

I could go on and on, but you get the picture. And if you're like the majority of women in America, you LIVE the picture! You know all too well what I was feeling, because you have felt the same thing! Of course, having so many children added to our situation, but almost everyone we know is too busy. Lord, deliver us! We need to learn to draw the line and say no at some point! No matter how others judge us! In fact, Tracy and I faced lots of judgment because we didn't let our children get involved in everything or go into town for lots of activities, but we were simply trying to survive!

While working on the rough draft for this book, Mother's Day 2002 was celebrated. I told Tracy that all I really wanted was for him and the children to leave for a few days! I wanted to be alone! I didn't want to have to pack or travel to get my solitude, either—I just wanted the rest of them to disappear for just a little while. I could eat what and when I wanted, watch the movies I liked, read, sleep, and just not have to be responsible for anybody else for a short break!

Well, that didn't really work out the way I'd planned. The following summer I DID end up with some time alone, sort of. We only had four of our eight children at home, and they were all involved in things that took them away from home. Benjamin was on a mission trip to Peru at the same time Ashley was on a mission trip to New Zealand. Anna, who was six at the time, was at my dear friend's, Coleen Yocum's, for Camp Cody (a camp she put on for her grandchildren, and was kind enough to invite my Anna to join!). That just left Justin, so he bounced back and forth between several family members for about four days, off and on. Tracy was still home nights until the last day, when he traveled to Texas with our youth pastor to pick up the mission kids.

Mind you, I didn't spend the time sleeping in, eating chocolate, and watching chick flicks! I worked on this book instead! It was a wonderful time with the Lord, though, reminiscing about how He brought Tracy and I through some tough times and blessed us beyond what I could have hoped for! I also had time to pray fervently for my children, so it was good.

Still, that last morning, after being alone during the night and knowing I had only a few hours left of solitude, I began to weep. I was just so overwhelmed. I began to pray out loud, since nobody was around to hear me. I thanked the Lord for my family—let Him know how grateful I am that I am NOT alone! Yet my heart was crying out for His help! How could I possibly do everything I felt I needed to do? The summer was already more than half over, and I hadn't even begun to finish the projects I'd lined out for the break. Since I was teaching school again, I had only two and a half months to "catch up" at home every summer before it all started over again. I was already behind—I hadn't planned to teach the year before, only agreeing to take the job one week before school started. This meant that the projects I had already put off during the previous summer, thinking I'd do them while the kids were in school, had already been put off for nine months.

The craft/game/sewing/junk room was so full we couldn't even walk through it! My recipes were disorganized and crammed into a cabinet—couldn't even find what I wanted. All the closets were disasters. I had pictures of the family that I'd taken for the previous year and a half that needed to be put into albums. I hadn't changed the family pictures on our walls for over six years—there weren't even any pictures of Anna up at all! Thankfully, she didn't even realize her picture was missing, because she looks almost exactly like her oldest sister, Sara, looked at the same age! Her baby book was about four years behind and needed updated. My bedroom needed an overhaul.

Tracy was remodeling one of our three bathrooms, another bathroom was next in line, and we wanted to tear out the carpet and refinish the wood floors in our living room. The house needed a deep cleaning so I could stand to even live in it! Plus it was looking like I was going to be moved at school from teaching first graders to going back to teaching junior high English and history—my first love as a teacher, yet requiring summer preparation in order to do a good job! Not to mention building our home-based business that was at a crucial time to really grow!

Add to that trying to finish at least the rough draft of this book, parenting four children, developing relationships with our grown children and their spouses, spending time with our grandchildren, mentoring some women I was teaching in Bible study (how to love their husbands!), and trying to be a decent friend. I was also supposed to exercise, eat right, plan menus, cart kids to their lessons, and find time to play with the children and have sex with my husband! It was overwhelming!

So I cried and asked the Lord how I could possibly do what I needed to do. I didn't get any answers then—sorry! But I did sense His presence and comfort. We can only do what we can do in any given day. We all only have twenty-four hours to spend, and it is not possible to get any extra hours, no matter how hard we try. So with the Lord's comfort came a knowing that I was NOT going to get it all done, and that was okay. I just needed to readjust my priorities and lists and goals and make the best of how it all turned out. School would start and I would not feel ready—I wouldn't be organized like I wanted, and my house would not be clean and our clothes wouldn't be sorted and mended and ironed and . . . you get the picture. But I would get up each day and trust the Lord to somehow make what I do count for something!

That's what it means to "redeem the time." We buy it back—make it worth more than it seems possible. We team up with the Lord to have it count for eternity, which lets us use the time twice, actually! We use it once here, and we accomplish something eternal that makes it count again! That is something we can't do on our own, but as we give our days to the Lord and keep serving Him, He will help us do something worthwhile. It isn't always preaching or writing a book or teaching a Bible study or Sunday school class! Sometimes it's just smiling at someone who is hurting or giving a hug or encouraging a child to keep trying. Sometimes it's sharing what we have with someone who has less. It might be opening our homes or visiting the sick or those in prison. Maybe it's giving clothing to the naked or food to the hungry. Perhaps it is interceding for the lost or sharing a Scripture the Lord has placed on our hearts. It might be spending a few minutes just worshipping the Lord for His goodness!

Many people shake their heads and tell me they just couldn't do what I do. Well, that might be true and it might not be true. I don't know where they are in life, and I'm not so sure that they really KNOW what I do! Even if it looks like I get more done, it doesn't mean I'm doing it all *well*! Something has to suffer when we divert our attention to so many things, so I'm not under any delusion that I'm Super Woman! Far from it! I do know, however, that we are not all called to the same thing. Remember the verses that liken the church to a body? Some of us are hands, some feet, and so on! But Jesus is the Head and He gives gifts as He sees fit to bless the body and reach the lost. Each one is important, and I probably couldn't carry anyone else's load, either! Jesus wants us to carry *His* load, for He says it is *easy* (Matthew 11:29).

There was a time in my life when I thought I *was* Super Woman! Many of us were fed a lie back in the '70's. Remember the fragrance commercial for Enjoli? That woman could "bring home the bacon, fry it up in a pan, and never, never let him forget he's a man!" We were sold the idea that we could have successful careers, have a family, live in a *Better Homes and Gardens* house, and keep our marriages vital—IF we wanted to. We were also told that the marriage part of it was optional—we didn't need men so much, after all! Women today are going home from the workplace in droves, because we're exhausted and needy and we've seen through the deception!

I know during busy times that I still need to rest! Yet I also know I have been given much, and the Word tells us that to the one who is given much, much is also required. I will have to answer for how I've spent my life, and so will you. Jesus will separate the sheep from the goats someday, and He has a lot to say about the activities of each! How we spend our personal twenty-four/seven matters! (See Matthew 25) Still, He gives His beloved rest (Psalm 127:2). When my head hits the pillow, I'm out like a log! I used to read for hours at night, but those days are over! I read myself to sleep, which usually takes less than five minutes, then drop the book and wake myself up! It's nuts!

So what about us gals? What about our needs for rest and peace? What about soaking in a bubble bath, taking walks, reading, resting, and so on? What about fellowship and friendships? *What about me?* Jesus said, "Whoever loses his life for my sake and the kingdom's will gain life!" But that doesn't mean He wants us to work ourselves to death! Maybe in other parts of the country, this concept isn't something you can identify with, but here in the Midwest, we have a very strong work ethic! Break? Who needs a break? The CEO of my company is fond of saying, "I'm going to work like there's no tomorrow—I can sleep when I die!" Well, that may be true, but if you don't get adequate rest, you'll die sooner! Plus you'll be cranky and heavier and less effective AND you'll have huge bags under your eyes! So go ahead and take a nap or leave a chore and go on to bed.

And at our house, we finally decided that the busy lifestyle we've lived for so long had to go. So I'm home again instead of working full-time. Some women can juggle both family and full-time career, but it doesn't work for us right now with the "extra" things we believe I need to be doing, such as speaking to women and writing and singing. We just couldn't reconcile our busy schedule with missed time in the Lord's presence. Sometimes we have to give up something good (my teaching at our Christian school) for the best (time to minister to the Lord, my family, and women).

When we're too stressed out and busy, we can remember Isaiah 28:9-13. The Lord doesn't want us to "do and do, do and do, rule on rule, rule on rule, a little here, a little there. . . ." He wants rest for His people! It has always been His will! He wanted it for the children of Israel, but they missed out on entering His rest because of their murmuring and complaining! True rest comes to those who find contentment in following Him! Isaiah 30:15 says, "In repentance and rest is your salvation, in quietness and trust is your strength."

Improving health boils down to some basic principles: drink more water—half an ounce for every pound you weigh, exercise thirty minutes a day—and breathe while you're doing it, balance your carbs and proteins—eating more veggies and fewer breads, and get enough rest—at least seven hours a night with as many before midnight as possible. Here again, having an accountability partner who really cares can make all the difference. And anything we do in the right direction is progress, right?

But all that aside, we will never get away from the premise I've stated over and over in this book: everything really goes back to Jesus—loving Him and knowing He loves you and being content in Him. He meets our needs! Nothing else does! Not men, not food, not perfection—only Him!

Usually we are much more concerned about our appearance than our health, which is probably the influence of our culture affecting us. We spend LOTS of money as a nation on cosmetics, lotions, potions, weight loss products, plastic surgery, liposuction, varicose vein removal, work out equipment, ETC. Do you know what makes us most attractive to our husbands, though? A submissive spirit! A wife who doesn't fuss and criticize! A woman who can get along without arguing on everything! A woman who shows some concern for someone else's needs! How many men have left their wives for women who weren't nearly as attractive physically? They leave for someone who shows some kindness and attention! No matter what natural beauty and gifts the Lord did or didn't give us, ANY of us can become the kind of woman our husbands will be drawn to! Instead of continually thinking about getting our own needs met, we can begin to minister to theirs and be the helpers God created us to be. You can't buy that in a bottle!

12. Damsel in Distress

As a child, I used to watch a cartoon titled "The Perils of Penelope Pit-stop." She was a true damsel in distress and got rescued several times every Saturday morning. I can still hear her screaming, "Hay-ulp! Hay-ulp" in her southern accent! What a far cry from what is expected of women today—we aren't sure exactly how to behave in this self-reliant society we are part of!

In Zechariah 1:15, the Lord says, " . . . but I am very angry with the nations that feel secure . . . ." One of the greatest sins is self-sufficiency. God created us to have a balance of relying on Him and others along with being able to take care of ourselves. For example, if we are healthy, we should not need someone else to come over and make dinner for our families every evening. (Of course, if we're busy and we can afford a cook or maid, bring her on! Ha!) If, however, you're a typical wife or mother, it's still necessary from time to time to be able to either have the rest of the family pitch in preparing the meal, or better yet, just eat out!

But if you're anything like me, you live precariously between being just FINE without anyone's help (thank you very much!) to being totally needy. Sometimes it's as though I'm wearing a flashing neon sign on my forehead that is screaming, "Somebody save me, notice me, take care of me, love me!"

Sometimes I think *nobody* loves me, but it's simply not true. Emotions are fickle and NOT a good indicator of reality. Worrying about whether or not I can locate one person to truly love me is self-centered living that leads to misery! But when we're wrapped up in our own pain and we haven't yet discovered that Jesus is the One Who came to heal us and be all we need, then we can't see any further than that.

We've all known people who come across as confident and aloof—maybe even a bit snobby. Yet when we get to know them better, we often discover a person who is just hurting, someone who has carefully erected walls of protection to avoid rejection. I've met women like that who ended up being very close friends as we shared enough personally to get past the hard exterior down to the soft, precious person under the pain.

With our husbands, though, we wives often think that we are exactly on target as to what our husbands are thinking, feeling, planning, and so on. We think their actions prove what we've believed all along: that they don't love us! This is nothing new; people have always projected their own attitudes and fears onto the actions of others around them!

Still, the marriage relationship remains the hardest one, perhaps because it is so daily. It can seem that we have plenty of evidence—hard, cold facts—to support what we "know" to be true about our husbands. We can think they really don't care about us or love us, and we have "*proof!*" Here's a list of "factual" evidence to show the lack of love:

He hasn't spoken to me all day except about the family responsibilities we must carry out.

He hasn't kissed me today.

He hasn't made love to me for (however long), even though I have humiliated myself by letting him know I want to.

He won't pick up his dirty laundry from the bedroom floor, even though I've asked him repeatedly to do so.

He didn't say anything about the special dinner I prepared.

He just sits and watches television while I'm dealing with the children and house.

He escapes to the garage to another project in order to avoid being with the family.

The list can go on and on, and each of us has our own favorites. Even though there might be an element of truth to what we are seeing, it still isn't the entire picture. Days, weeks, months, and even years can go by with no obvious changes. We feel unloved and rejected, and yet our poor husbands often don't even realize there is a problem, and if they are aware of something amiss, they still usually don't know what it is nor how to fix it. Sometimes our perception of the situation we're in shows itself in faulty logic like this:

Nathan is tall.
Nathan is a man.
Therefore, men are tall.

Notice the jump from one conclusion to another? Yet we stake our lives on the belief that we have accurately evaluated how our husbands treat us!

Consider this scene found in the book of Esther. Evil Haman was out to destroy Esther's people, the Jews, because he was jealous of her cousin, Mordecai. Mordecai refused to bow down to Haman, so Haman devised a terrible plot to kill the Jews, never knowing that Queen Esther was also a Jew.

Mordecai asked Queen Esther to go to the king to expose the wicked scheme and to save her people. It was no small thing for her to enter the king's presence without being summoned; she risked her life to do so! The king was pleased with her, though, and heard her request. She invited the king and Haman to a banquet, where she simply invited them to another one the next day. She promised to reveal her petition to the king at the second banquet.

In chapter seven, we see the king and Haman dining with Queen Esther at the second banquet. The king asks her again what her request is, saying he'll give her even up to half of his kingdom. She asks the king to spare her life! She explains that she and her people were going to be slaughtered and annihilated! The king demanded to know who would dare to do such a terrible thing, and Esther replied that the adversary and enemy was Haman!

> *Then Haman was terrified before the king and queen. The king got up in a rage, left his wine and went out into the palace garden. But Haman, realizing that the king had already decided his fate, stayed behind to beg Queen Esther for his life.*
>
> *Just as the king returned from the palace garden to the banquet hall, Haman was falling on the couch where Esther was reclining.*
>
> *The king exclaimed, "Will he even molest the queen while she is with me in the house?"*
>
> *As soon as the word left the king's mouth, they covered Haman's face." (Esther 7:6b-8)*

Haman was hanged on the gallows he had built for Mordecai! But my point is that the king did not perceive correctly what was happening when he saw Haman leaning towards the queen. Molesting Queen Esther was FAR from Haman's mind! He was just trying to figure out a way to save his neck!

Another example is found in I Samuel 1:12-16. Eli observed Hannah praying, but he only saw her lips moving without any sound coming out. He concluded she was drunk, and he even rebuked her for it! She had to let him know that she was just deeply troubled, not drunk!

There are many other examples throughout God's Word, as well as in our lives. The sad thing is, we often jump to conclusions based on what our eyes or ears tell us, but we can be wrong—dead wrong! We don't always evaluate the information correctly, perhaps because our past experience or fears or pain slant it.

How many times have our husbands genuinely tried to show us love, yet we've rejected their attempts due to a misconceived idea of their motives? How many times have we made wrong accusations? How often have we missed a blessing simply because we were unwilling to consider the heart motives of our spouses?

Christmas break of 2001, I was feeling exhausted and achy from overwork and the effects from fibromyalgia. It's a disease in the arthritis/immune system family, affecting the muscles around the joints. I seldom ask Tracy to do things for me personally—only for the household in general, such as running to the store, making a deposit, helping Anna get ready for bed, etc. But I let him know during Christmas break how run down I was and how much I needed a good massage. I was picturing a deep, hot oil rubbing that would soothe my achy muscles and relieve some tension. I thought it might lead to further intimacy, which was fine by me! I mentioned it two or three times, but the break went by without any attempt on his part to minister to me in that way.

The weekend after break, I had taught for two days, and I still felt totally tensed up in my neck, shoulders, and lower back. I knew we really couldn't afford a professional massage, yet I hated to ask Tracy again to do it, since I had already made my needs known clearly. I had also been back to see my doctor about the pain I was continuing to experience even a year after my hysterectomy. He had suggested that Tracy and I have sex more often, and I thought it was a fantastic idea! I had joked with Tracy about having to follow doctor's orders, but that didn't make our busy schedules change overnight! We had only had sex twice during the busy holiday month of December, and I was feeling frustrated and unloved.

That particular Saturday morning, I can't even remember what comment Tracy made as he started to get out of bed, but whatever it was, it set me off. I made a rude comment to him about him never having sex with me, either. "Either" meaning besides all the many other ways he let me down that I just hadn't brought up—yet. I was cranky and hurt, and I had resorted to my old game of accusing and disdain to try to get my point across: that he was falling short of meeting my needs.

Tracy tried to make up with me, but I couldn't receive his love in any form at that point. I finally blurted out that I was in real physical pain, yet he didn't care enough about me to help. To me, that could only mean that he didn't really love me.

I hurt, he could help, yet he wouldn't or hadn't in all those weeks, so what else *could* it mean? Understand that when my emotions aren't involved, I can look at situations objectively and draw more accurate conclusions! But at that time, all I could perceive was my pain.

Tracy felt horrible about not having rubbed my back yet, and he offered to do it. I felt all the old need rising up within me, yet a huge wall was erected that wouldn't allow his love to enter my heart. I hated even having to ask him to rub my back in the first place. Then for him not to follow through was a slap in the face. I didn't want to have to bring it up more than once, which felt like begging; it made me feel unworthy and unloved. I couldn't even receive the back rub from him once he was willing to give it, and the misery in our bedroom was tangible.

Persisting, Tracy asked me to *please* let him rub my back, and even though it was exactly what I needed, my pride wouldn't let me welcome his help. We were at an impasse, and neither of us knew what to do. I was weeping, he was frustrated, and both of us knew we had other things calling for our attention, so we couldn't just stay in the bedroom all day accomplishing nothing.

Suddenly, in a moment's time, the Holy Spirit showed me what was happening. I could see that my independent spirit had developed over years of feeling like I had to take care of my own needs. I simply didn't believe anyone else would! I began to see flashes of my childhood, being the oldest of six children in a home where my mother worked hard just to keep all of us intact. New babies came every two years until I was six years old, then another one in four years and the last one four years later.

My mother loved me then, and she loves me now! I am not placing any blame on her or my father. There are no perfect parents, and having eight children myself, I know firsthand how difficult it is to even skim the surface of meeting their needs. Somebody gets left out, no matter how hard you try. Mama used to say that the squeaky wheel got the grease, and it is so true: the children who are demanding attention tend to get it, especially when it's a crisis! It doesn't mean you love the others any less; they just seem to be okay, so you deal with the matters that are most urgent.

Since small babies obviously have great needs for attention, I believe early on I developed the idea that I needed to be independent and do what I could for myself. Not only did Mama have smaller children to deal with, but she also had the extra burden of trying to make our family work in spite of

Daddy's alcoholism and frequent extended absences. When he was home, he spent his weekends, and sometimes weeknights, going out with his drinking friends. Mama needed help, but she wasn't getting very much. In my own young mind, somehow I felt I should not burden her any more than necessary. I began to believe, *even though it might not have been founded on what was true*, that if I didn't take care of myself, nobody else would.

Through the years, I developed an independent spirit that wouldn't allow me to rely on others. My past experience had taught me that it was better not to let anybody know my needs, because if they didn't come through for me, it would hurt. It would be an indication that they must not love me. If I had a legitimate need, but the other person was not willing to meet it, then there must be something innately wrong with me—something that made me undeserving and unloved and unworthy and unwanted. I built strong walls around myself and did whatever it took to take care of myself so I would seldom have to face the possibility of finding out someone else didn't find me worthy of love. It was self-protection.

This realization of how I had learned to depend on myself came to me in just moments, and I began to sob uncontrollably. Tracy waited patiently, holding me while I let the pain seep out through my wails. When I was finally able to talk, I began to share with Tracy my new understanding. He could see for the first time in twenty-five years of being married to me that it was a huge step of vulnerability for me to even ask him to do something for me!

The real clincher was this: I had believed all those years that *Tracy* was the one who had intimacy issues! I thought he just didn't know how to get close to me, and that he wasn't trying to be romantic. Yet I could see clearly that I was actually the one who refused to *let* him get close to me! That Saturday morning, for the first time, I finally let someone else in. I exposed myself and my needs, and I allowed Tracy to take down some of the walls securely fixed around my heart, and I received his love. We had the most intimate sharing of our lives, and I was totally amazed at how comforting it was to let someone else truly minister to me. It was risky, to be sure, but he was there for me. The effects of that morning are still being felt, and I am amazed at the freedom that is coming as we change the way we interact with one another.

With my newfound understanding, I have reflected back to a time before my daddy passed away. My sister Cathy lived in Texas, and she was close to giving birth to her last child, Isaac. I was also pregnant with our last one, Anna. Most of our family had gathered during Christmas break at Cathy's house, and Tracy took our children back to Kansas while I stayed to be with Cathy for her baby's arrival. My parents were there for the birth, too, and we were thrilled to welcome little Isaac to the family. I planned to stay a couple of days, then fly home.

One evening while we were visiting, my mother arranged to meet some of her siblings for dinner. I had been close to the younger aunts because we were near one another in age. In fact, Mama's youngest sister, Carol, was only nine months older than I. I began to get excited about the gathering, but hours were ticking by, and Mama didn't invite me to go. She said she figured Cathy wouldn't want to go, since her baby was brand new—but she didn't even mention me. I kept waiting for her to ask me along, but it didn't happen. She didn't give a reason for not inviting me, and when she and Daddy left for the evening, I was crushed. I cried for hours off and on, and I felt totally rejected and unloved by my mother.

I tried to figure out why she wouldn't want me along, but there just wasn't a reason that would let me balance the scales, no answer that would let me conclude that she found me worthy or that she loved me. It was a deep wound that festered for months after we went home, and it reopened issues that I thought had been put to rest years earlier.

I had believed for a long time that Mama favored two of my siblings over the rest of us kids. Both had experienced traumatic teen years, and it seemed that Mama was closer to them. She even seemed to like their children more than the rest of the grandchildren. I always tried to understand and be "big" about it, but it still hurt.

All these thoughts were tormenting me. Finally, I knew I had to talk to Mama about the rejection I was feeling from her. She was surprised and hurt, yet I had to find out why she didn't love me as much as she loved the other two. If she didn't want anything to do with me, I felt I could deal with it, but I just wanted to know why. What was it about me that she didn't like? What fault in my character kept her from wanting to be with me?

Her answer was a shock to me then, but after the revelation I had with Tracy on that recent Saturday morning, it is even more astounding: she said that I just always seemed to be fine. I didn't seem to need her, but they did. I came across as self-assured and all together and independent, so she just didn't feel needed. The other two needed her greatly, and they showed it. The truth was, I *also* needed her greatly, but I didn't ever feel like there was enough of her to go around for all of us, so I just took care of myself the best I could. Both of us were missing a blessing!

Is this an indictment of my mother or her parenting skills? *NO!* Rather, it ties right back into the main point of this book: there is not a living person who can meet our deepest needs! There is a place of need in every person born that only the Lord Jesus Christ can ever fill! Our parents will fail us, our spouses will fail us, and our friends will fail us! We will fail them, too! There is only *One* Who can be all we need Him to be, and He is waiting to do that right now for each of us. He is the Living Water that will quench our thirst and make us whole and complete.

Mama and I worked through those rough months, and today we are closer than ever. We're both busy, but we always enjoy our time together as a special treat. I am learning to let my walls down in other relationships, too, and it is amazing what the return is as I let others into my life to a deeper degree.

I used to get canker sores in my mouth—really bad ones that would give me great pain for several days. I would have two or three at a time sometimes! My dad told me that if I would pour salt into them and leave it there for a few minutes, the canker sores would dry up and heal. I was desperate enough to try it, but totally unprepared for the pain! Through the years, I modified the treatment and simply gargled salt water to promote healing. I learned something about the healing power of salt, though, from the experience. True, it hurts and burns like crazy when you first use it, but it really does an effective job of speeding up the healing process. It stings at the time, but leaves the wound or sore feeling somewhat numbed and far less painful than before treatment. It is worth the pain!

I believe that the Lord sometimes pours salt into the areas where we are wounded. Even though it hurts at the time, it also dries up the source of the original pain, leaving us better than we were before He began His own personal treatment. In this area of true intimacy and connectedness in my life, I could tell that He was allowing the pain so that in the end I would hurt much less—and even have times when I didn't feel any pain at all!

The Lord Jesus tells us in Matthew 11:28-30, "Come to me, all you who are weary and burdened, and I will give you rest. Take my yoke upon you and learn from me, for I am gentle and humble in heart, and you will find rest for your souls. For my yoke is easy and my burden is light."

The Word tells us that it rains on the just and the unjust. Things happen to everyone, Christian or nonbeliever.

We cannot automatically assume that the Christian will be spared pain or suffering; in fact, just the opposite is true. Jesus said that no servant is greater than his master. Since He experienced suffering, we will, too!

John 15 tells us that Jesus is the vine and we are the branches. The Father is the husbandman or gardener. He prunes the branches that are bearing no fruit, but if we abide in the Lord Jesus, we bear much fruit. What we need to realize is that the Father uses the same tool to prune or trim some branches that He uses to cut off some others. The circumstances that come our way can either make us or break us; it depends on where we are abiding and what our focus is. We can cooperate with the Lord's work in our lives and learn lessons the easy way, or we can stubbornly refuse His lessons and experience more pain.

Gary Chapman's books on the five love languages are classic, and the truths he shares have helped me get a better picture of Tracy's motivations. Chapman explains that people give and receive love in different ways based on what he has termed their "love languages." He classifies them as acts of service, words of encouragement, physical touch, quality time, and gift giving.

Tracy's love language is acts of service, and he shows love by doing things for me. It's also how he receives love, and it took me years to realize that he'd much rather have me fill his dinner plate for him than leave him a love note! Before we learned these concepts, I used to get irritated if he hinted that he'd like me to serve him this way! I figured that God gave him two legs, and he could use them! After all, I'd already been slaving away in the kitchen for hours preparing the meal!

His "escaping" to the garage also irritated me before I understood it! The example Tracy grew up with played a part in forming the way Tracy interacted with the rest of us. His dad was much older than his mother when they married; he was thirty-three and she was only sixteen! He also had an extremely passive personality, so when that was coupled with his lack of youthful energy, he had very little to offer Tracy when it came to time spent together. Tracy also fights this passivity and finds it more comfortable to work in the garage to avoid real contact or intimacy with us. Since he has a fear of failure, too, it is easier to do a project that he knows he can do well than to face possible failure in relationships with his family.

But finally seeing past my own love languages, which are words of encouragement and physical touch, I could begin to minister to his needs in a way that would clearly express how much I appreciate his hard work; it's how he's declaring his love for our children and me. Having learned how much he also needs input, I wrote him a note on his 8th anniversary at his current job.

June 21, 2002

Dear Tracy,

I just wanted to tell you again how much I appreciate you and your hard work. Nobody I ***ever*** *dated could have—or would have—taken care of me like you do.*

You faithfully go to work day after day, toiling relentlessly, even without the recognition or promotion you deserve.

I recognize you! My cup is full of joy as I see your love for me and the kids poured out in your labors every day.

Thank you. I love you more than life.

Yours always,

Becky

Okay, you're thinking that he'd probably rather have had me wash the Suburban or bake him a pie, and you're probably right! But I needed to show my appreciation and love the way I speak it, then I also tried to be sure it was coming through in a way he could hear and receive it, so I took treats and a big balloon to him at work to share in the break room.

So often I take him for granted! A little appreciation and respect can go a LONG ways toward keeping love alive, and how we *perceive* our mate's actions makes all the difference. Sometimes I still want to ask, "Where is the back rub? The kiss? The handholding? The romantic note scribbled on toilet paper in the morning?" He does try to do those things, but I know in my heart that he is *shouting* his love for me every time he picks up a hammer, plunger, or wrench, and I can receive it that way now instead of thinking he's always trying to escape!

Last year we experienced yet another situation where I was playing the needy dame and expecting Tracy to speak love to me in MY language. We were having another nice, long Christmas break, Tracy with one week at home and the children and I with two full weeks. We went into the time full of expectations, but his and mine didn't necessarily match! (You might be picking up on a theme for these long breaks! Maybe finally spending time together brings things to the surface! Ha!)

Tracy felt he was showing me great love by spending over three days, which included most of his birthday, putting together a new computer desk he had bought me for Christmas. He also fixed various things around the house and moved pictures for me—stayed busy almost his entire break, not counting the holidays.

I was aggravated with him for not paying attention to me! I wanted loving words and gentle backrubs and pats on the bottom as he passed by! I wanted lingering conversations in the mornings over coffee and gazing into each others' eyes! I wanted soft music and candles and romance at night! Unfortunately, my crankiness with him did not effectively communicate my desires!

I used a double standard, too. I expected him to understand why I was crabby; not only was I not getting the romance I needed from the time we spent at home, but I also felt frustrated that there was so much to get done. I still had so much weighing on me: lessons plans, semester grades, menus, thank you notes to my students for their Christmas gifts, writing and preparing to mail a newsletter for the year, organizing the office once the desk was done, working on this rough draft—not to mention the regular chores of running the household! He was supposed to be patient with my crabby attitude, while not reacting negatively to the unrealistic expectations I was placing on him! But I didn't want to give him any grace for crankiness or falling short of my expectations, even though he had more to do than he could finish during the break, too. I wanted to fully express how he had let me down—drama queen that I am!

Truth is, it is better to be *kind* than *right*! Pride isn't a fruit of the spirit; *love* is! Look at I Corinthians 13, where love is described. We cry over how little we think our husbands show us love, but if this portion of Scripture defines love, how are we measuring up *ourselves*? Do *we* keep no record of wrongs? Do *we* always believe the best? Are *we* patient? Do *we* seek our husband's needs before our own? Do *we* always protect? Always trust? Always hope? Always persevere? Do we ever fail? In light of the truth, we must admit that all of us fall short of loving perfectly. And since *we* do not love perfectly, why do we expect our husbands to do so?

I know, many of you are probably thinking, "I'm not asking for him to love me perfectly! I'm just asking for some sign of life! Just a kind word here or there would make such a difference!" I understand! Remember, though, we are not trying to make our husbands do what is right, and we are not looking for happiness in our relationships with them. Rather, we are working towards changing our *own* attitudes so that we will be closer to Jesus and more like Him! Part of that is exemplifying the fruits of the Spirit, which includes walking in love towards others. Our husbands are others! If we claim to love God, yet we don't love our brothers (even our husbands!), we are lying! (I John 4:20)

Waiting for God to answer or help us can seem long and hard, and we can fear a lifetime of nothing ever changing. We can do nothing to change the past. We can't change the people in our lives, either. We can't even change ourselves with anything that is worthy or lasting! The bottom line is, we need Jesus! He wants to heal those areas where we have been hurt, and we all have them. He wants to help us up out of the pit we're in. He wants to set us on a road full of purpose and life! The past matters, because it affects the present and even the future. So we don't want to just ignore what has happened to us then. But we do need to get His healing and perspective on it, forgive those who harmed us, and move on.

Even when we're doing our best, the progress can seem slow and it can be easy to take matters into our own hands. Think about Abraham. When he was still Abram and Sarai gave him the "brilliant" suggestion of going in to her handmaiden, Hagar, he fathered a son named Ishmael. This was not God's chosen plan for Abram and Sarai! After that poor choice, Abram had to wait *thirteen years* before the Lord even spoke to him again about the covenant He had with Abram! It was another year before Isaac, the child of covenant, was actually born. The Lord is not slow in doing what He has said He will do, and we need to wait patiently on Him. Striving will only bring us pain, as we've seen in the war that has gone on between the descendants of Ishmael and Isaac, the Arabs and Israelites, all these centuries.

Waiting on Him will renew our strength and help us grow. The journey is as important as the destination, remember?

We used to sing an old song from the '60's, "It's my Party, and I'll Cry if I Want To"? Well, I have thrown many major pity parties on my own behalf, believe me! We usually think of self-pity as the type of "emotion" that is lowly. Actually, it is a proud thing! It says, "I deserve better than this." Intrinsic to its survival is the idea that I am "good" and others are not treating me according to that standard. Sickening!

We live in a society that is full of victims! Someone else is to blame for everything that is wrong with us! We take very little, if any, responsibility for our own actions or attitudes or words. We focus on how we've been wronged instead of putting out some energy to try to make things right! The fact is, everybody has been wronged! That is just the effect of living in a sinful world. Without meaning to minimize anybody's pain, I still have to say that we really do need to work through it and proceed rather than wallowing in our sorrow.

Some people really do have it harder than others. I think about my adopted children, whose birth father killed their birth mother. That was tragic! Worse than most of us will ever even imagine, much less experience. But I knew we would cripple the children for life if we let that tragedy make them think they deserved special treatment. Yes, they've had major issues to work through, and they saw a counselor for a long time. But those who have done that hard work of facing the issues are continuing to heal and becoming whole.

Self-pity wants to be perceived as our friend, but it is an enemy that needs to be fought! It won't just go away on it's own; it will hold on and kick and scream! We need to do battle against it with the truth! Psalm 65:8 says, ". . .where morning dawns and evening fades You call forth songs of joy. . ." No matter what our circumstances are, we have reason to rejoice and sing praises! As we look for the good and glorify the Lord, self-pity flees! It can't stand worship and a thankful heart! So if you battle that particular enemy, begin to spend time each day in praise and worship—it will kick self-pity in the teeth!

In fact, everything that comes out of our mouths has a huge impact on how our lives are lived! The Bible tells us in Proverbs 18:21 that the power of life and death are in the tongue! When I was telling you that sometimes I think nobody loves me, I didn't mention that my friend Coleen told me to quit saying that! Repeating it only gave power to the enemy to reinforce it; my agreeing with it gave him permission to keep me from finding fulfilling relationships!

The same is true when we badmouth our husbands or continuously talk about what we don't like about them. What we say matters in the spiritual realm! Begin to say good things about your husband, your marriage, your ability to love and respect your husband, and his ability to love you and provide for you. Change the way you speak and you'll change the way you think and act!

The Word tells us that we are supposed to be like Jesus. Well, according to Romans 4:17, He calls things that are not as though they are! Go ahead and thank God for the good qualities in your husband that you desire! Thank Him out loud every day for the way He made this man! Look for ways to build him up! If you belittle him or complain about him, those words bring death to him and your relationship. That doesn't mean to internalize pain, because it will surely show up in some form! But truly, from your heart, begin to exercise faith by what you say! Begin to thank God for him! Remember the qualities that first drew you to him! It is unlikely that *everything* about him is rotten! Keep a notebook of the sweet things he says or does for you so you can remember them when the going gets rough! Watch the Lord change YOU as you change your attitude!

One day when I saw Dr. Phil on the Oprah show, he was scolding a man who was blaming his lack of attention towards his wife on her intense neediness. In this man's mind, everything was her fault because she expected and needed too much. The truth is, her needs were legitimate! Yet who wants to live with a needy, distraught person? Who wants to face the insurmountable task of trying to fill that gaping need?

Wouldn't it be wonderful if we could all—husbands and wives—have our needs met by Jesus? Think how peaceful our homes would be! What unity! What blessing! We wouldn't be seeking to have our own needs met, but we'd be content, looking to bless the rest of the family! That IS God's plan! And He longs to bring us joy even in the midst of hard circumstances. Psalm 84 tells us, "Even when we go through the Valley of Baca (weeping), we make it a place of springs."

So what do you do if you know your husband won't live that kind of life? You do it, anyway! Let it start with you! What do you have to lose? What is the worst that could happen if you were to get your needs met by the Lord and begin to truly minister to your family? If your husband doesn't reciprocate, have you lost anything? No! He wasn't doing it before, either! And you are free! Your family ends up being blessed! The Word says that the ungodly husband MIGHT be won by the conduct of his wife! There is no guarantee of that happening, of course, because he has a free will. But YOU will be blessed beyond imagination, and you will have the peace that comes from knowing you have done all you can in the situation. We simply must quit expecting our spouses to give something they are incapable of giving—not because of any flaw in them, but because our true needs can only be met divinely. The longing we have inside is for Jesus! And He is willing, waiting, and ready to fill that heart cry!

If you have never asked Jesus into your life, now is the time. Simply let Him know that you realize you are incomplete without Him. Confess to Him that you cannot come into the presence of God—that you realize you are not worthy, because of your sin. Even if you have not done anything really "bad," such as murder or stealing, you have still fallen short of perfection. Ask Him to cleanse you. Let Him know you believe that when He gave His life, shedding His blood, it was good enough to pay for your sins. Ask Him to forgive you, based on your acceptance of Jesus' payment for those sins. And ask Him to come into your life, filling you with His Spirit and His life and His love.

If you *have* asked Jesus to come into your life before, but you still have a sense of dissatisfaction or need, now is the time to ask Him to forgive you for looking somewhere else for contentment and fulfillment. Let Him know that you need Him as much today as you did the day you invited Him into your life. Ask Him to fill you with His Spirit of love, and let Him know that you need Him to meet your needs. Tell Him exactly what you're feeling—all the fears, the loneliness, the heartache, the anger—and ask Him to cleanse you of all the junk. Open your heart to Him and let Him prove Himself to you. He really *is* enough! Let Him show you!

Really—right now, stop reading and invite Him to take you to a deeper place with Him, and ask Him for His strength to do your part in seeking Him. His Word promises that if we seek Him, we will find Him!

So, gals, when you are feeling like crying, "Woe is me," just remember that there *is* Someone Who loves you, Someone Who is waiting to meet every need. When life is difficult, as well as when life is at peace, He is constant. And His "rescue" is just a prayer away!

13. A Mighty Fortress . . . Is our God!

Castles of old were actually fortresses—forts built to protect royalty and often even the common folk from their enemies. They were places of refuge in the midst of the battle. A stronghold is also a strong place or fort or fortress. Used in that context of being a refuge, it is a good thing. We all face battles and need a place of safety and protection.

But there is also a type of stronghold that is harmful to us. I would love to believe that I don't have any harmful strongholds in my life—that Jesus has taught me the truth about my own sinful nature and I have learned to be a submissive wife and all is well on the western front! But the truth is, for SO many years, I constructed my *own* protective walls. These strongholds that we build ourselves by clinging to old ways of thinking, or that we allow our enemy to erect in us, are not a good thing. We allow certain things to get a "strong hold" in our lives, and we actually then forfeit our opportunity to see the Lord be our Protector!

II Corinthians 10 talks about those negative strongholds in our lives. Look at verses 3 - 5. "For though we live in the world, we do not wage war as the world does. The weapons we fight with are not the weapons of the world. On the contrary, they have divine power to demolish strongholds. We demolish arguments and every pretension that sets itself up against the knowledge of God, and we take captive every thought to make it obedient to Christ."

We see that first of all, we aren't fighting the same way the world fights. They fight each other; we begin to realize that much of our battle takes place in our heads! We actually need to fight ourselves, so to speak, as it relates to fighting the old patterns and habits of thinking.

We want long-term change, not just short-term promises. So we have to be willing to see where we are hard and unbending, where old habits of thinking have hindered our growth. Strongholds in our own lives are so hard to see. They are often quite obvious to others, but I know I need the Lord to reveal mine to me, because they cause destruction to Tracy, our children, and me. I need to deal with them instead of making excuses and defending my harmful habits of acting and reacting in certain ways.

Some of my strongholds have been dealt with and are gone for the most part; I don't even struggle in those areas anymore. Probably someday, when the current ones are all obliterated, the Lord will show me new areas where He'd like to free me, too! But for now, I still struggle with resentment, having a critical spirit, and trying to control people and circumstances, even after all the progress that has been made. Let me show you how the battle is still being waged in these areas!

During the writing of this rough draft, when Tracy was remodeling one of our bathrooms, we faced some challenges. He is meticulous! As a machinist, he measures parts to the thousandth tolerance; his work has to be perfect for all intents and purposes. Naturally, when he's working on projects at home, it's the same thing! He gets out his level and tape measure, checking everything continuously to try to make it exactly right.

Several times during this project, I wrongly compared Tracy with my dad. Daddy might not have made it perfect, but he'd have had the bathroom done in one weekend, two tops! True! But Tracy did a beautiful job, and the work should last for years.

Unfortunately, I get stretched to the limit while waiting for the finished product. I bite my tongue, encourage his efforts, and try not to be too needy! We lose him for weeks upon weeks (and months upon months!) when he's doing these projects, and it's a strain on everyone. He does the work himself for several reasons. First, it's far less expensive than hiring someone else to do it. Next, he does a better job than many handymen would do! Finally, we don't always know what we want until partway through the project as we see how it's coming along!

Anyway, at one point several weeks into the bathroom makeover, we were all tired of the project, but just hanging in there. Well, one night he showed me a light fixture he had purchased for the bathroom. It was pretty, but I was concerned that it was too big. This bathroom is rather small, and I didn't want the eye to travel to the ceiling! We had purchased a really pretty three-mirrored medicine cabinet that I liked and thought was a nice focal point for the room, and I felt the large ceiling light would be distracting.

I told Tracy I thought it was too big, but I was trying not to be pushy! I hoped he would not use it, but I wanted to let go and not worry about it; after all, it was just a light!

I played a game with our children while he went ahead and put up the light. Sure enough, when he showed it to me, I hated it! It dominated the room! I tried to be tactful, but I felt I needed to also be honest. So I told him it was really too big for the room. Well, he reacted strongly! I know he was tired, so he sure didn't want to hear that I didn't like it after he'd spent such a big chunk of time installing it! So he said it was just too bad—the light was staying up.

My eyes watered up, which I hated! I wasn't trying to manipulate him with the tears—I just couldn't stop them! Trying to keep my composure, I told Tracy that I would not bring it up again, but I just wanted him to know that I totally disliked it and would be distracted by it every time I went in the bathroom. He retorted, "Good! Don't bring it up again!"

I cried for several minutes, but tried to just let it go and act nice to everyone. It wasn't just that I didn't like the light; it was that all the time he had spent trying to make the bathroom perfect was now ruined with one item that didn't have to be used! He was being stubborn, but I wanted to have the right attitude. I guarded against self-pity, because the "voices" in my head were already busy, telling me he just didn't care about my opinions, he was the most stubborn man on earth, it wouldn't hurt him to just make it right, etc. It was a struggle!!!! I kept playing with the kids, having to let go over and over again in my mind.

A few minutes later, Tracy came in behind me and started rubbing my shoulders. He apologized for being hard, and he told me he'd try to do something else with the light. It took a LOT for him to humble himself, but since I had not insisted or acted bratty to him, he had the freedom to change his mind without looking like a wimp. He knew I had made a huge effort not to fuss with him, and I knew he had to totally humble himself to apologize and change it. Years ago, we would have had a standoff that could have lasted for days. I would have been openly disrespectful, and he would have shouted and been rough with his tools and slammed doors—maybe even broken the light fixture!

What other kinds of things cause resentment to surge? What can reduce me to shouting criticisms about what Tracy is doing wrong? What tempts me to take up the reins of control again?

Well, for example, when Tracy wants to work on a project instead of going to church! (The roof comes to mind!) I have to let go and just do my part of helping him instead of trying to "help" him see what he needs to be doing! The Lord is in control of Tracy and his spiritual growth, too! He is able to let Tracy know if he's doing the wrong thing! I won't help by interfering with that! Besides, who knows what kind of fellowship the Lord might have with him up on that roof?!

Sometimes Tracy expects our daughter Ashley to take better care of the youngest one, Anna, than he does when I'm gone or busy! Responsibility issues surface, and I blow! I think I know SO much better than Tracy how our children should be reared!

In November of 1999, one day in church, Tracy was doing something that distracted me—biting his nails! In a note, I nicely asked him to stop, but he wouldn't read it. That hurt my feelings! I wrote again to him, pretty much forcing it under his nose, saying, "You might as well have slammed a door in my face just now." He wrote back, "I will read it and be loving, but you are distracting me from hearing the Word." Naturally, I was really irritated now! I wrote back, "Which is what *you* were doing to *me*. And *now* even more. Don't make excuses for your attitude! If I was fidgeting [something that used to drive him crazy—I continually kept time to the music going on in my head by tapping on his legs, etc.], and it distracted you, *you'd ask me to stop*. And because I *care* about you, I'd *want* to stop. I'd try. I'd want you to keep telling me when I was doing it again, because I'd *want* to quit for you. When the tables are turned, you get upset with me for letting you know when something you're doing is distracting me. That makes me feel like you *don't* care."

He apologized later, but I have to admit that I find it disgruntling at times that often he and other men are defensive about anything that they perceive to be criticism. So much of that has to do with the horrid attack on men in our culture. They are made out to be total idiots, and they really do feel the need to defend themselves. If they were secure, they wouldn't need to protect their egos so staunchly. But I let that kind of thing cause yucky stuff to resurface in my own heart.

Also when I feel unwanted, disrespected, unloved, and lonesome, it's easy to be prickly to protect myself. Resentments from my childhood resurface, but it's so subtle, I direct it all at Tracy. He takes the heat for years of unmet needs that occurred before he and I ever met!

Of course, there are times when he IS the one at fault! For example, he usually doesn't do anything for Mother's Day until the last minute—if that. In 2001, he still had done nothing by Saturday evening, even though I had suggested a massage or a new outfit from Kay Lane's Closet. I went ahead and bought some things there for myself earlier that day since I knew he had done nothing! I had suggested that he have the kids make breakfast for me Sunday morning, because I wanted them to feel like they had done something for me for Mother's Day, but instead he made breakfast for me himself. Nice gesture after the fact, but not what I wanted or what they needed. I felt *he* wasn't honoring me in their eyes or teaching *them* how to honor me and show love. It hurt and I believed the lie—that he didn't love me.

Mother's Day 2002, I planned a cookout for both of our mothers, and we invited my siblings, their kids, and all our married children. It was fun, but again he did nothing for me. No present, no card, no breakfast in bed.

May 15, 2001 Okay, three pages of this [griping and recording my pain] is enough. I need a way out of this pit of despair, though. It's been too long since we were in harmony. According to Genevieve [Daughters of Sarah], I need to let go of this and be thankful. I need to look to the Lord for emotional needs. I need to confess my resentment and forgive Tracy. She says the Lord understands what I'm feeling.

Okay, Lord. Please take all this yuck and help me lay it down. I can't do it on my own. Help me be at peace with Tracy, because YOU are meeting my needs and YOU care and YOU are in control of his growth. Help me not to pick it back up.

Isaiah 37 Don't tell me my God can't or won't deliver. He WILL!

And this mess in our marriage is such an attack. Right now when the Lord is leading me to pray for our ministry, or maybe it was already there and needed to come out. Either way I want cleansed and free. Lord, help me know how to act tonight.

May 17, 2001 Tracy was very sweet yesterday and wants to work together on making our marriage all it can be. He really does have a lot of perseverance and tenacity, and I'm thankful for that. I know the enemy hates us and hates the family and wants to hold us back from fulfilling God's plans for us to lead others, but he can forget it! We will move on in faith!

May 29, 2001 I woke up feeling resistant towards Tracy today—and he wasn't even here! He'd already gone to work! What does that say? That I had harbored some offense and slept on it. I allowed myself to feel a slight irritation that he didn't go swimming with us or play cards with us . . . etc.

Good grief, he's doing things I've wanted done for years! I can't have it both ways! He needed to work while he felt he could. The kids and I are all off for the summer, but he isn't! I need to remember that! I need to die to my own ideas and expectations today, release him from "owing" me anything, and look for ways to bless him.

And then there are times when he hasn't done anything wrong at all—I just feel downright cranky about living a life of submission! I think there's no way I'm going there, so Tracy just might as well back off and watch what he says to me! It's awful! I much prefer days when I have a deep sense of peace, knowing it's the right way to live!

God has given us the power to pull down those things that have had a strong hold on us for years! The release is often immediate; the habits of thinking, acting, and reacting still need to be changed, though, and sometimes that part of being free can take a little longer! But it is possible to be released from the old ways that hold us back. We actually pull down and demolish those thoughts that do not line up with the truth of God's Word! We can learn to insist that our thoughts line up with what is right and make our thoughts obey the Lord! Since the battle is taking place in our minds with thoughts, and thoughts are formed with words, what better to use than the truth of the Word of God to fight back! This takes practice and diligence! But the pay off is SO worth it!

In my particular case, solving the authority question made everything else much easier! I had already made Jesus Lord of my life, and that included being willing to submit to Him and His will for me. He IS Lord, whether we accept Him that way or not! Someday every knee will bow and every tongue will confess that He is Lord! (Phil. 2:10) Only when we accept that Lordship into our own lives do we experience true freedom. Realizing that the same is true of my husband and the position of authority the Lord has given him has taken longer! But Tracy is the head of our home whether I accept it as so or not! It is true even if he himself doesn't accept the role! He will be accountable for how he leads, and I will be accountable for how I submit and accept his leadership.

Discontentment with that arrangement is a trap! Those thoughts are sin! They need to be brought captive, cast down, and rebuked! When I am critical of Tracy, thinking he's wrong, that he's shirking his duty to lead, that he's goofed off instead of being diligent, etc., then I must reconcile myself to obedience simply because to do otherwise is sin on my part. I must reject thoughts of criticism, resentment, resistance, and so on. I need to be pliable and let the Lord work in me, trusting Him to take care of Tracy and where he is in this journey. I have a full-time job just to submit my own heart and thoughts and life to the Lord! If Tracy isn't right or sincere, the *Lord* will deal with him!

I'm most miserable when I'm basing my attitudes and actions dependent upon my opinion of whether or not Tracy is doing his job right! Ugh! There is nothing Tracy can do to make it okay for me to pick up the reins of control again! The Lord can do a better job of building Tracy into the man He wants him to be than I can! Amazing!

Sometimes we come to an impasse; we can't seem to get past our hurt feelings or pride or sense of being wronged. We know we need to forgive and release the other person, yet we can't seem to find the way to do it. I know I have experienced KNOWING I need to forgive and not let the sun go down on my anger, yet finding I can't seem to do it! I am trying, and I am asking the Lord to show me a way out. Someone else in the same situation might be thinking that's ridiculous; you simply decide to forgive and go on! It's not always that easy, especially if you come from a long heritage of unforgiveness!

Also, since I took a vow that I would never allow a man to treat me the way I saw my father treat my mother, then I have a problem reconciling the accounts in my head! If I forgive Tracy for yelling at me or losing his temper or neglecting me—or whatever the offense happens to be—then I am going against my promise to myself! A promise that became a stronghold in my life! It can take me quite awhile to work through all of that in my head! Many times, when I have found NO way out, I have finally just asked Tracy to pray.

Here's the crazy thing: then I get mad at him for not already thinking of praying himself! That critical spirit takes over and I disdain him for not "leading" spiritually—*obviously*, we have a problem that we need supernatural help with! Yet I only thought of it myself moments earlier! What a hypocrite I can be! But God is so patient and answers us anyway! I am always amazed at what happens when we stop to pray! Inviting the Lord into every area of our lives is exciting! I've seen Him bring peace and even joy to situations for us that moments before seemed big enough to cause us to split up!

What if your husband isn't a Christian or he won't pray, even if you ask him to? Then don't ask him to! Do it yourself! Even if he WILL, you need to do it yourself! Prayer is one of the important pieces of equipment the Lord gave us, and it works like nothing the world has to offer! I have to laugh when I think of all the things we try first, because it's ludicrous! I could have saved lots of heartache if I'd been willing to turn to the Lord instead of following the pattern I was used to: fighting till Tracy gave in! That can take a while, too, believe me!

As much as the devil wants to destroy our marriages and homes, the Lord wants to heal them, and even more! There's a chorus we sing at church that goes, "In the presence of Jehovah, God Almighty, Prince of Peace, troubles vanish; Hearts are mended in the presence of the King." So true! He specializes in bringing healing to our hearts, and He delights in giving us answers that bring peace!

This is true in every area, not just marriage! Any relationship, any situation, any threat, whatever we are going through, He wants to be a part of! God really does want to be involved intimately in our lives, even the details. Taking all of it to Him makes all the difference, even if at first nothing changes except our own perspectives and attitudes! There can be peace in the eye of the storm when we are wrapped in the Lord's love and protection!

Too often we just react to our circumstances instead of taking them to Jesus. There is an old hymn of the faith that encourages me to seek God's help: "Take It to the Lord in Prayer." One line goes like this, "Oh, what peace we often forfeit; oh, what needless pain we bear, all because we do not carry everything to God in prayer." We would see tremendous answers if we would just invite Him to participate!

In addition to prayer, I find that confessing what is true helps me when I'm struggling with forgiveness or if unity is elusive for Tracy and me. Sometimes he has apologized to me, but it seemed less than convincing, like he was blaming ME for whatever is wrong; at those times I need extra help! I can either say it to Tracy or just out loud to myself that regardless of my feelings, I am standing with him, submitting to him, etc., and I trust the feelings to follow. He, too, can tell me that his confession towards me is he truly loves me even when it doesn't look like it, and although he can't meet all of my needs, he can and will meet some of them! Saying so accomplishes much, because there is power in the tongue!

Sometimes I have to back down instead of forcing an issue to be resolved right now! Especially if the enemy can catch me exhausted and sleep-deprived, so that I'm not in my right frame of mind—he knows half the battle is already won. Throw in a husband who is also too tired and overworked, and you have a recipe for real trouble! While it is true that we don't want to let the sun go down on our anger, it is also true that sometimes trying to work out a disagreement is best left until after we've had some sleep! If we can somehow agree to love each other and agree to disagree for awhile, then often we can rest on it, think things through, pray for attitudes, and come back together to have a fruitful discussion!

We are both a work in progress! Yet both of us appreciate the changes in the other one SO much that we are encouraged to keep working towards cooperating with the Lord to change ourselves, too! We know we're dealing with another human being full of ideas and opinions and habits that usually don't match our own! We know we're both married to another sinner! But we are growing. And even when we aren't perfect at this, we are trying and making steps in the right direction.

Instead of growing discouraged with what we perceive to be our spouse's slow progress or our own, we can take encouragement from Isaiah 43:18-19 "Forget the former things; do not dwell on the past. See, I am doing a new thing! Now it springs up; do you not perceive it? I am making a way in the desert and streams in the wasteland." We must believe this for our husbands and marriages! Don't dwell on our husband's past mistakes! (Even if the past was just a week ago!) God is doing something in them! It's crucial to forget how they have been before—don't let it hinder our ability to believe for something new! The Lord never lets us down! Even in areas where there isn't even a trickle of hope or life, the Lord will bring streams! He will do it!

At any rate, I know that even when Tracy hurts or disappoints me, which is inevitable, it can be strategic to reminding me that I can't depend on people. There is only ONE who can meet my needs. He's the only One Who can really love me unconditionally and perfectly. The walls I built for myself sometimes did help protect me from harm, but even when they did, they kept out the good blessings, too. I'm trading those for what the Lord has to offer. He is a high tower of protection, and He wants to wrap His protection around me in love. He is the One Who can keep harm from actually getting through to me, yet let love in to touch me at the same time. We can call out to Him like King David did in Psalm 61:1-4: "Hear my cry, O God; listen to my prayer. From the ends of the earth I call to you, I call as my heart grows faint; lead me to the rock that is higher than I. For you have been my refuge, a strong tower against the foe." That's true even when the foe turns out to be ourselves!

14. Happily Ever After

At this writing, Tracy and I have been married for twenty-seven years. We decided to celebrate our new-found hope and love by renewing our vows for our twenty-fifth anniversary. It was marvelous! We finally got the hippie wedding we'd wanted the first time around!

We held the ceremony at Carey Park in Hutchinson, Kansas, outside just like we'd dreamed of! Tracy wore a tie-dyed shirt and blue jeans. I wore a tie-dyed long dress with a huge daisy printed on front. I wore my hair down with a wreath of daisies crowning my head. Seven of our eight children joined in the ceremony! They wore blue jeans and white shirts and the girls all wore single daisies in their hair.

They formed a line on one side of me while I sang and played my guitar. We were waiting for Tracy to walk across a bridge to join us. I had always wanted to do it this way, because in reality, we the bride, the church of Jesus Christ, are the ones who are waiting for His return to get us, not the other way around! So we reflected that truth to start our ceremony and cried our way through the vows we wrote to each other:

> *Pastor Kelly: Twenty-five years ago, Tracy Spencer and Becky Yates made a commitment before God to be joined as husband and wife. They met on January 3rd, 1976, and Tracy knew the day he met Becky that he wanted to make her his wife. He kept it a well-hidden secret for a long time, though! Becky was engaged to someone else at the time, and Tracy had suffered a painful breakup, so he was in no hurry to try to make anything happen. He admired Becky from afar while their friendship grew. On June 18th of that same summer, he asked Becky to be his wife. Since they hadn't had even so much as one date, she thought he was joking at first! She told him she would have to pray about it, then took him to meet her parents. Tracy and Becky's dad spent the entire first afternoon that Father's Day sharing the Lord in her backyard. It was the first time Becky and her dad had even liked the same guy!*
>
> *Just days later, Becky told Tracy she would marry him. They were engaged for three short months, and married on Sept. 18th, 1976. The Lord had given Tracy a Scripture on which to base their lives: Colossians 1:17 which reads, "He is before all things, and in Him all things hold together." They had this Scripture printed on*

the napkins at their wedding because they knew that Jesus was their only hope for a marriage that would last.

As is true with every married couple, there were some hills, as well as some valleys. There were dark times, times of disagreement, and times of temptation. There were seasons when they didn't even like each other very much! Both had much to learn about what it meant to truly love another human being so much that they were willing to give up their own rights and desires in order to please the other. It was hard going for many of their first years together.

Tracy and Becky meant what they said when they asked Jesus to hold them together, though. They stayed together even when the world would have told them to give up. They trusted in Jesus even when they had nothing in common but Him. They found that He was more than enough!

Today they desire not only to renew their commitment to each other, but also to celebrate the love the Lord has given them for each other, and His keeping power. Truly, by Him all things hold together, and we are joined as witnesses to praise the Lord as they embark on the next season of their lives together.

Tracy: Twenty-five years has been great, and now looking to the future, I affirm to you that my love for you is undying. I will always seek for your good and seek God for His best, no matter what life brings our way, for His love holds us together.

Becky: Tracy, I am amazed at how quickly the years have flown. Seems like just days ago we were first committing our lives to each other, full of hopes and dreams, praying for a life of joy together as we served the Lord.

And now, somehow twenty-five years have come and gone! I am almost amused when I look back to who we were then, and the lessons the Lord has taught us since we first said, I do."

I didn't know what it meant to really love someone else unconditionally. My heart is sometimes grieved when I think of the many times I rejected the love you wanted to show me. I am so thankful that you were willing to stay with me, even when I was proud and hard and unloving. You loved me through my selfishness and showed me the kind of unconditional love I needed. Since you first loved me, I was eventually able to learn to love you, too.

Sometimes I don't know if it was your strength of commitment or just plain stubbornness that caused you to press on when I was thinking only of my own needs, while overlooking yours. The selfishness I showed to you was so far from love . . . yet you stayed with me and kept caring. Not very many men would have been able to see past the ugliness with the ability to keep hoping for love to be returned. Even when my heart was unfaithful, you didn't give up.

When I think of what that has meant to me as a woman and as a wife, I am blessed beyond words. When I think of what that has meant to our children, who have a stable, loving home now, I cry tears of joy to our heavenly Father. Thank you for being an example of His father's heart to our children and His lover's heart for me.

I know life will not always be easy in the future, any more than it has been in the past. I know hard times will come; sad times are inevitable; and irritations will sometimes get the best of our dispositions during stress and overwork. Yet I find no greater joy in this stage of our lives than walking through it all with my hand in yours.

When we first said our vows, I didn't even know what it meant to submit or obey you as the head of our home. But I have learned that God is able to lead our family through you, so I willingly, lovingly embrace the peace that is ours as we walk in His order for our home.

Nothing could compare to the joy you have given me by standing by my side as we have parented our beautiful children. The laughter and tears and fullness they have brought to us as a couple have been worth it all.

But as those years pass and we look ahead to each of the children leaving home, I want you to know that I am totally excited about our time alone together. There is no one else I would rather spend those years with!

You have faced adversity and your own shortcomings head-on. You have shown me the tender side of your heart and you have persevered through hardships. Many would have run, but you stood and fought and got the victory. I will always admire you for that.

You are the one I want. You are the one I respect. You are the one I love.

I give you my heart and my life. I trust you to cherish me and care for me. I promise to keep loving you more every day and to stay by your side no matter what comes our way.

I commit myself to you again, forever. I would choose you again, without a doubt. I love you, Tracy Spencer. Thank you for loving me.

(You see who the wordy one is in this relationship! Ha!)

Pastor Kelly: Tracy, Twenty-five years ago, you took Becky to be your lawful wedded wife. You promised to love her, to cherish her, to take care of her no matter what life brought your way. You promised to be faithful to her alone. Do you still commit to love her with that kind of unconditional love?

Tracy: More than ever before, I do.

Pastor Kelly: Becky, at the same time, you agreed to love and respect Tracy. You promised to let him lead your home as you obeyed him and helped him, even when the inevitable difficulties of life pressed in. Do you still commit to love him with that kind of unconditional love?

Becky: More than ever before, I do.

Pastor Kelly: The commitment you made before God was binding twenty-five years ago, and it is still in effect today. Yet God has heard your desire to publicly say again that you promise to love and cherish and respect each other, living together until one or both of you join the Lord in eternity. May your commitment, marriage, and love be blessed with a double portion of God's most precious grace as you go forward today.

We sang to each other and enjoyed the prayers of our family and friends who gathered around us. Then we had a reception, complete with 70's music and surprising each other with songs we had prepared especially for each other. We took a trip to Oklahoma City and enjoyed being alone while our oldest daughter watched the four youngest. Thinking about it now still brings a huge smile to my face and lights up my eyes with love for him!

Tracy also made me smile—even though tears were streaming down my face—after we read Eric and Leslie Ludy's book about their courtship, *When Dreams Come True*. Tracy was moved tremendously to apologize to me for how our courtship went. Eric and Leslie were SO pure in the way they treated one another, and it is a beautiful love story! But it made Tracy realize all over again that he had not been a leader during our early years. He was getting a glimpse again of the pain that I suffered during that time, and he was genuinely sorry. The more we learn the truth, the more we have to face regrets. Of course, I was touched by his tenderness, and I had to also apologize to him for falling short. I felt, though, that I also needed to let him know that the Ludy's have a message of purity for their generation, which is awesome and SO needed! But *we* have a message for *our* generation, too! For those who have NOT had a storybook romance, there is still hope! You can still find a love beyond your greatest dreams! It is not too late to change!

Of course, all of this I'm sharing has come from years of walking with Jesus! This much change does NOT come overnight! Knowing Him and loving Him and serving Him is a lifelong walk! But it is a journey that is worth giving all we have! Start today, knowing it will take your entire life to know Him, but that it will be a life well spent!

There are people who go through life never changing, never maturing, never "getting" it. How sad! I love this stage of life because I've learned a few lessons along the way! If I were still struggling with the same issues I faced in my twenties, this stage wouldn't be much fun. But so many things are settled in my thinking! I'm content with Tracy and our life together. I'm trusting the Lord with my children and grandchildren. It's a good life.

Eight years ago when I was facing the fact that middle age was upon me even though I was expecting a baby, I penned these lines in my journal.

> *November 18, 1995 I'm thirty-nine years old today. If I were to compare my life to the seasons, I'd say I* ***should*** *be in the autumn of my life. I'm definitely not old, so winter is out! Fall has always been my favorite season. I love the colors, the crispness of the cool, snappy air, raking leaves, traces of spring and summer fading and falling to be collected as mulch to get us through the winter.*

Even as the leaves fall, I realize my physical home—this body—is beginning to fall, too. I noticed new wrinkles on my neck yesterday. My cheeks are starting to sag, as is the rest of my body.

My memories are a source of joy and comfort, vivid at times like the red and orange of fall, more muted other times like the browner tones, but all covering me like a protective blanket.

As I think of my oldest daughter leaving home this year, it's another reminder of the autumn of my years—my children, too, will begin to "fall" from the tree.

The experiences of real life have robbed the idealism of youth, forcing me to begin to say goodbye to summer. Having a terminally ill parent also forces me to realize that the chilly snap in the air is just a precursor to the harsh cold of winter, yet it isn't here yet, and I'll enjoy the few "weeks" of autumn I have left.

Even as I write, though, this new life inside me is stirring, rolling, kicking—perhaps turning a somersault! It's like an unexpected gift of summer—like days blowing in, refusing to let autumn settle in quite yet, warming up at least the afternoons with carefree days of throwing off jackets and having a few last picnics, softball games, and swinging at the park.

Yes, it's autumn in my life, but summer is still within reach and winter doesn't seem as dreadful as I thought it would be now that I'm here."

No matter what stage of life you are in, it will be made richer and fuller by a closer walk with Jesus! Life is so short! Let's make our brief journey through it count for something eternal!

Dear sister, if you think your marriage can never be complete, please hear me. The Lord wants you loved! He's not against love; in fact, there are some great love stories in the Bible! Proverbs 30:21-23 reads this way: "Under three things the earth trembles, under four it cannot bear up: a servant who becomes king, a fool who is full of food, *an unloved woman who is married*, and a maidservant who displaces her mistress." (italics mine) The Lord *wants* you loved by your husband, deeply and completely. Since it is His will, you can pray in faith for it to happen! You might say, "Well, you don't know my husband." I say, "Then you don't know my God!"

We don't change in order to manipulate heaven. We change to be like Jesus and please the Lord. Because He's good.

Because it's right. Even if our husbands never change. BUT we can also expect it from God! Not putting expectations on our men, for it's more than they can give. But looking to the One Who loves us most.

Think about it: He *commands* husbands to love their wives! So we can pray according to His will! Then we can expect an answer. We don't feel sorry for ourselves and wallow in self-pity when we don't see results. Instead we thank Him for our husbands and His plan, then cheerfully do our part and wait on Him. We know that kind of attitude pleases Him.

If it seems that Jesus isn't enough, then you simply have not met the "real" Jesus! Perhaps your concept of God has been colored by how you perceived your earthly father. Perhaps your past includes some type of spiritual abuse that has given you an untrue picture of God's nature. Please, don't depend on those images of God to suffice! Ask Jesus to show you the depth of His love for you! John 8:30-31 tells us that if we continue in God's Word, we will really be His disciples and we'll know the truth that sets us free! Learning Who He is and how to walk in His ways is a lifetime endeavor—not something we achieve instantly! Give Him a chance to show you His love really is the answer you've been looking for!

The Lord really *does* love you! And He is really enough! Yes, He wants to use people and relationships in your life, but if none of those *ever* work out, He is still enough! Think of the many ways He loves you!

He loves you like a perfect father. You don't have to earn it! He will take care of you without your doing anything to deserve it, simply because you are His child. Even if you are "naughty," He won't withhold what you need. Would an earthly father withhold food or shelter from you if you wrote on the wall? Of course not! You might have to scrub the wall or go without your crayons for a couple of days—or you might even get a swat! Your needs, though, would never go unmet. Your sin does not change God's love for you! He will do whatever it takes to bring you back to proper boundaries, and He's not in too big a hurry. He wants you to obey out of love, not fear, and if you'll listen to His words, you won't have to face hard consequences nearly as much!

He promises that He will take care of you if you are His! You will be clothed better than the lilies of the field and fed better than the sparrows. He knows what is best for you, too, and He doesn't make any "rules" that are not for your good! Just like an earthly father makes rules such as not crossing the road without looking both ways or eating your vegetables or saving the candy for after the meal, all in your best interest, so also the heavenly Father is thinking only of what will do you good, not harm. When He gives rules about marriage, adultery, fornication, divorce, etc., it isn't to keep you from having fun! It is to protect you and give you the best chance at fulfillment and happiness possible.

He loves you like a big brother! He's been where you are and understands, so He gives you grace. He wants to give you advice and warnings about dangers ahead so you can avoid making common mistakes.

He loves you like a true love! This love is unconditional! Read through Romans 8:35-39! When you're up, down, okay, not okay, pretty, ugly, crabby, happy, and so on, His love remains true. He says that *nothing* can separate you from His love—not even your own sin! He sees the best in you and understands you. He enjoys little things about you that other people might not even notice! He gives everything for you. He wants to be with you all the time. He is jealous of other loves in your life!

The wedding feast of the Lamb is coming. Jesus is returning for His bride! You are His bride if you have accepted Him into your life! He will toast you, take you, and love you. Nobody else can love you like He can. Nobody else can meet your needs like He can!

He loves you as your God! He is love itself! He sees the finished product you will be, having eyes of faith and high expectations. He wants you to succeed and be all He has created you to be! He wants good for you and is able to change you from the inside, out. He is forgiving!

"I wait for the Lord, my soul waits, and in his word I put my hope. My soul waits for the Lord more than watchmen wait for the morning, more than watchmen wait for the morning. O Israel, put your hope in the Lord, for with the Lord is unfailing love and with him is full redemption. He himself will redeem Israel from all their sins." Psalm 130:5-8

Photo from Becky and Tracy's 25th Wedding Anniversary Renewal! Look at those "hippies"!

The King's Proclamation

(Okay, this is really the appendix, but once again, I just wanted you to be sure to read it! I thought you would enjoy hearing from Tracy!)

I held Becky's letter to Gene in my hands and felt numb. My mind was clouded. My heart was clouded. My eyes were clouded as the tears blocked me from seeing any more words on the page. I was hurt.

At first I was angry with both of them, but then I was just angry with myself. I quickly felt it was my own doing. I didn't see it coming and allowed it to get as far as it did. I blamed myself, not excusing their sin, but knowing I had let it happen by not meeting Becky's needs.

I was taken by surprise that Becky wasn't in love with me after being married for so many years.

I had been shut down for a long time. My own personal struggle had to do with feeling like a failure and feeling rejected. We had moved to another state, and we had four children and one on the way when we moved. We ended up having to move in with my sister-in-law and her husband and son just to make ends meet. Our finances were so bad that no decisions had to be made! Everything already had to be on a tight, tight budget. We ate lots of government food like commodity cheese, beans, or whatever we qualified for.

I believed the Lord wanted to use me in a ministry there. When that didn't happen, I felt like I had not succeeded at what God wanted me to do. I was disappointed with my ability to hear from God.

Besides the ministry, I had thought I would be able to make a good living there, but the economy was depressed. There were so many illegal aliens taking the jobs for lower wages. I worked hard for almost two years for my employer, but never got any praise for what I did. I lost lots of weight, giving my best at the physical labor, so I was so tired I couldn't put any effort into looking for a different job.

My boss would cuss me out and berate me. I was making more money than he would have paid someone else in my position, and when I stood up to the boss for how he talked to me, he and his son set me up so they would have a reason to fire me. The son had me fill out my time sheet incorrectly then they accused me of cheating them out of money! So they fired me! It was a pretty low blow. I was getting more disappointed.

Nothing was working out in the job situation, and we were in such poverty.

While I was swallowed up in my own shell, Becky was being successful at her job managing a KinderCare. She was fast, smart, and talented, and I felt inferior.

All of that had an affect on my shutting down and not trying to lead our family anymore; I finally just kind of gave up. I didn't desert God, but I was just hanging on to what was left. I took my old job back in Kansas, but even after we moved back, I was disillusioned with where we were and what we were doing. I didn't feel that God had let me down. Maybe I had been trusting His servants to open all the right doors and turn all the right keys.

I had always said I would never be like my dad. He was a very passive person who always expected my mother to take the lead about just about everything. He went to work, came home, ate, slept, then got up and went to work again. I was determined as a Christian that I would not be a passive man who let the woman lead. But all the experiences had me right where he had been: shut down, just going through the motions.

So I felt I was to blame for not being what Becky needed. We had already formed so many habits over the years and got used to each other the way we were. Our commitment to the Lord and the commitment we made to each other before the Lord was all I needed. I didn't need all the feelings. But I felt like I needed to demonstrate to Becky the kind of love she needed. We really began to work on our relationship at that time.

As our relationship grew, we began to adapt and fit each other. I was never accustomed to speaking loving words; I never really had loving words spoken to me that much. I never got them from my dad; my mother gave them to some degree. They really didn't have time to be intimate and find our deep personal needs. When Becky needed something to be fixed, I could easily do that, but that's my love language. She needed me to tell her how much I love her and to encourage her and give her loving touches.

Of course, I ended up doing something that really hurt her. My sin came between us even when it was unconfessed. I was struggling with my relationship with the Lord. I didn't feel deserving of Him. I felt like I would never measure up. Before I was "found out," I had already repented, but when Becky forgave me, it was like the Lord forgiving me all over again. It made his forgiveness fresh to me. I was overwhelmed by the pain of my sin, especially the suffering I put my loved ones through.

So much had made me feel like giving up, but I hung on to God's Word. I silently acknowledged that He was on our side. I couldn't turn my back on Him completely. If Becky had totally given up on me, I don't think I could have gone on. But she had the power of God to forgive me and start again.

I had to rebuild the trust and kind of "pay penance" for my sin as she interrogated me about everything I had done. But I felt it was no less than I deserved. I had totally undone any respect she had for me, and I was going to have to bear up under that. I was just glad she still loved me. I couldn't believe that she didn't decide to end our marriage.

I went to Promise Keepers in Colorado and other things like that to show how sincere I was about starting to lead our family spiritually again. In time Becky began to trust me again. She has that "stick-to-it-iveness" not to give up!

When things remind me of my sin, it gets hard. God forgets, but I don't, and I can get down. I have to look up, away from my sin. God throws our sin as far as the east is from the west. I have to remember that the sin is not *me*. God made me a new creation, and that has to be what I identify with. Not with the old, not with the sin. Only with what Jesus died for.

Becky has helped me build confidence. She brings it out in me. I love that woman! She's got a light in her eyes and heart. I've changed a lot over the years being married to her. I used to be locked up in myself. I'd be a social hermit, totally inward, if not for her. Her social "wellness" has helped me to be better with people. That's good, because God is a people God! If He's going to use me, I've got to be able to come out!

The love she has for God and for me is so powerful that I would be a fool to give up now! I'd be a fool not to put my best effort into our relationship to continue to make it grow, to find new and better ways to demonstrate love to her. I would not want to do anything else in my own life to cause her to move away from me or give up on me. When Becky displays love to me in spite of knowing all there is to know in me, that's showing me the same love Christ shows to me.

I've realized that my calling is really what I thought it was before, to teach and disciple young people. Only now it's my own children that God has given me, not through a church program!

I would say to women that if you know the power and love of Christ, then don't give up! Don't jump ship too quickly! Good can overcome evil! Thank God if it gets better and ask Him for help if it gets worse! Love covers a multitude of sins, so learn to forgive.

Men, guard your hearts and love your wives. Love never fails, so demonstrate it even when they are hard to love. Reacting will only complicate things. If you first show love, it will be a healing medicine. They don't need us to fix their problems; they need us to hear them and show we care.

I'm in this marriage for the duration! I made my vows before God and His people, and that's the way it's going to be!

Suggested Reading

Even though many people hate to read, it is still necessary to mental health! There is a wealth of information available that can challenge, encourage, and stimulate our thinking, helping us on the pathway to change.

It has been said that the person we are five years from now is largely determined by what we read today. Think of the significance of that statement! It is true for good and for bad. Sometimes we think that if we look at or read something "bad," it only affects us for the moment, but it actually becomes part of the fiber of who we are and who we become. Thankfully, that is also true for the good!

I highly recommend the following books to both husbands and wives, and of course, I hope you'll also want to read my other book and share it! It tells our story of how we were led to adopt our children, giving an honest picture of the challenges and victories we experienced. Good for those who struggle with perfectionism, wonder how to effectively serve God, or cry over hurting children. Some of these books can be purchased from my web site or at my book tables.

One of the best things Tracy can do to show me he really loves me and wants to work on our marriage is to read books on the subject! Thank you, honey!

Beyond Daughters of Sarah by Genevieve White
Cash Flow Quadrant by Robert Kiyosaki
Daughters of Sarah by Genevieve White (my favorite for women)
Every Man's Battle by Stephen Arterburn & Fred Stoeker (how to walk in sexual integrity—a "must read" for all men!)
Five Love Languages, The by Gary Chapman
Fool-proofing Your Life by Jan Silvious
If Only He Knew by Gary Smalley (especially for husbands)
Leapin' Lizards . . . and other leaps of faith by Becky Spencer
Making Love Last Forever by Gary Smalley
Next Trillion, The by Paul Zane Pilzer
Please Don't Say You Need Me by Jan Silvious
Power of a Praying Wife, The by Stormy O'Martian
Rich Dad, Poor Dad by Robert Kiyosaki
Shadows over Stonewycke by Judith Pella & Michael Phillips (fiction)
Sons of Abraham by Walter White (especially for husbands)
When Dreams Come True by Eric & Leslie Ludy (especially for singles or those who are engaged)
Women Who Love Too Much by Robin Norwood

Ordering/Booking Information

Becky is available as a speaker who especially enjoys teaching women how to love their husbands! (Yes, it can be taught!) Many women who had given up hope for their marriages have been encouraged and challenged through her ministry. She also likes to share her adventure in adoption and how to find your life calling. Consider having her come to share at your:

Church
Mother/Daughter Banquet
Retreat
Ladies' Organization
Civic Event

She is also available to sing at weddings, county or state fairs, and share her original music in concert.

You may order additional copies of this book or her music or other books by calling, writing, or visiting her web site. Price lists may be requested.

Becky Spencer
406 W. Ave. A
Buhler, KS 67522
(620) 543-6518
1-800-211-1202, ext. 14718
(leave a message with your return number)
beckyspencer@GoNowMail.com
www.beckyspencerministries.com

Most importantly, if you want to know more about what it means to know and serve Jesus Christ, please contact Becky! She would be honored to respond!